HOW I FELL IN LOVE WITH MY ANXIETY

ADAM KNIGHTS

BROWN DOG BOOKS

DEDICATION

To my anxiety: you magnificent, persistent, unwelcome house guest. Thanks for never leaving, even when I didn't answer the door. This book wouldn't exist without you – quite literally – because you kept me awake long enough to write it.

And to everyone who's ever Googled 'Am I dying?' at 3 am while their partner snored peacefully beside them … this book is for you.

TABLE OF CONTENTS

PART ONE

THE WAR YEARS

(How I learned that fighting your own brain is a terrible strategy)

INTRODUCTION

A NOTE FROM THE FRONTLINE

'You can't outrun anxiety. You can only outpace it with honesty and a touch of humour.' – Adam Knights

I'm writing this as a man who has finally kicked benzodiazepines out of his life.

If you know, you know.

If you don't, count yourself lucky and feel free to skip this paragraph.

For the rest of us, those little pills that promise calm but quietly deliver dependency – the ones accompanied by a voice that whispers just one more – are gone.

Evicted ... told to pack their bags.

It wasn't pretty.

But then again, nothing about this journey has been.

I've read stacks of books on anxiety: self-help manuals, clinical guides, programmes, mindfulness manifestos. Most are written by doctors, therapists, researchers – people who have studied anxiety from the outside, peering at it through glass like it's an exhibit in a zoo.

This book isn't like that.

This was written from inside the cage.

By someone who has lived with the bloody animal for decades. There's no white coat here. No clipboard. Just scars, stories and a dark sense of humour that kept me alive when nothing else would.

I'm writing this because I've learned something essential: I can't heal unless I'm brutally honest.

Not politely honest.

Not edited-for-public-consumption honest.

But uncomfortably honest – the kind that makes people shift in their seats.

Because here's the truth: you can't outrun, outsmart or medicate this thing forever. At some point, you have to look it in the eye and say, 'Right then, I suppose we're doing this together.'

So to my fellow anxiety sufferers – my people, my tribe, my fellow inmates in this peculiar prison – I want you to know this:

There is a way through.

It took me over twenty-five years of wrong turns, dead ends and spectacular face-plants to find it, but I did. And I'd like to save you some of that time. Think of this book as the shortcut I wish someone had handed to me – a map drawn by someone who's walked the territory, complete with warnings about the quicksand and notes on which bridges are dodgy.

What I'm sending you here is genuine, hard-won, been-through-the-wars love from me, and from my anxiety, which is sitting right here on my shoulder as I type this.

It just leaned over and whispered, 'Tell them we said hello.'

This isn't a medical book, and I'm not a doctor.

I was a soldier, then a businessman, and now I'm a bloke who spent years fighting his own nervous system and I lost every single engagement.

If you're in crisis, please talk to someone qualified.

What follows is just one man's journey from:

'Christ, I think I'm having a heart attack' to:

'Oh hello, old friend. Fancy seeing you here.'

Welcome to the tribe.

Let me start by telling you something that might sting a little: you're not special or unique.

I know your anxiety feels unique – the way your chest tightens at 3 am over something you said in 2007, your brain catastrophising over a routine dental appointment, or the memory of calling your boss 'Mum.'

But join the queue.

There are millions of us. You've accidentally joined one of the oldest, most resilient social structures in human history.

You've joined a tribe.

CHAPTER ONE

WELCOME TO THE TRIBE (AND WHAT IS A TRIBE?)

'You're not uniquely broken. You're normally broken. Like the rest of us. Welcome to the tribe.' – Adam Knights

Long before nations, corporations, LinkedIn networks or WhatsApp groups existed, there were tribes – and they worked. For tens of thousands of years, they were the operating system for human survival. And they were far more than a random collection of people in the same place.

A tribe is something older, deeper and far more powerful: a collective bound together by shared experience, mutual dependence and the unshakable understanding that nobody survives alone.

The classical tribes of Africa – the Maasai of Kenya and Tanzania, the Zulu of Southern Africa, the Himba of Namibia, and the San Bushmen of the Kalahari – understood something we have systematically forgotten in our rush to become 'independent', 'self-made' and 'crushing it' on social media.

They understood that belonging isn't a luxury. It's a survival mechanism.

HOW A TRIBE ACTUALLY WORKS

The Maasai don't wake up each morning thinking, 'Right, better check my individual quarterly objectives.' They operate on principles that have kept their people thriving through drought, colonialism and the aggressive expansion of Kenyan tourism.

Shared identity: Every Maasai knows who they are, their age set, their clan and their role. There's no existential panic about 'finding yourself' because the tribe has already told them where they fit and that they belong. Belonging is not something to earn; it's a given.

1. **Collective responsibility:** When a Maasai warrior is hungry, the village feeds him. When he's wounded, they heal him. When he's being difficult, they tell him. Nobody is left to struggle alone, and nobody pretends they don't need anyone.
2. **Rites of passage:** The Maasai, like the Zulu and countless others, mark life's transitions. You don't quietly age into adulthood while your parents wonder if you'll ever move out. You are initiated, you are recognised and the tribe witnesses your

transformation. The message is clear: You are one of us now.

3. **Shared suffering:** Here's the uncomfortable truth: tribes don't bond over brunch or book clubs. They bond over hardship. The San Bushmen track game across the Kalahari for days, sharing exhaustion and the eventual feast. The Himba endure drought, displacement and the daily grind of desert survival together. Struggle isn't weakness, but the glue.
4. **Reciprocity:** You give what you can and take what you need. The Zulu concept of ubuntu – 'I am because we are' – isn't a feel-good slogan. It's an operating principle. Your individual identity is inseparable from your community. You do not exist in isolation.

WHAT A TRIBE FEELS LIKE

I spent nine years in the Parachute Regiment – the British Army's elite airborne infantry. We're the blokes who jump out of perfectly serviceable aircraft and run towards trouble while everyone else runs away.

Here's something about tribes that most civilians will never truly understand, and it has absolutely nothing to do with race, religion, colour, background, education or where you grew up. Nothing.

There's a brutal selection process in P Company that earns you the right to wear the maroon beret. Nobody cares whether you're from a council estate in Salford or a manor house in Surrey. Nobody cares what God you pray to – or whether you pray at all. And nobody is interested in your A-level results or your father's profession.

They care about one thing: can you be relied upon when everything goes to shit? That's it. That's the entire entrance exam for true tribalism.

The Parachute Regiment taught me that a tribe is forged under pressure, not in comfort. You don't build unbreakable bonds over tea and biscuits. You build them when you're exhausted, cold, hungry and genuinely uncertain whether you'll make it through the night.

You build the bonds when the bloke next to you – the one you might not even particularly like – becomes the only thing standing between you and failure.

I served in Belfast and East Tyrone during the Troubles. I operated in Africa's Rift Valley. I spent time in the jungles of Borneo with the Iban tribes. Everywhere I went, the principle remained the same: the tribe makes you stronger than you could ever be alone.

When I was lying in a godforsaken ditch in Northern Ireland, waiting for something to happen, the man next to me wasn't defined by his postcode, his accent or his skin colour. He was defined by whether he'd hold his nerve when the moment came, whether he'd drag me to safety if I got hit, and whether I could trust him with my life.

That's a tribe. Everything else is paperwork.

The military understands something civilian society has

largely forgotten and that's individuals break, but tribes endure. No matter how fit, brave or well-trained a single soldier is, he'll eventually reach his limit. But a section, a platoon or a regiment – bound by shared purpose and forged under pressure – can achieve the impossible.

I've seen men who were genuinely terrified, find courage they didn't know they had – not because they stopped being afraid, but because they couldn't let the tribe down. The fear was still there, but belonging was stronger.

Common goals. Shared hardship. Mutual reliance. The understanding that your survival depends on the man next to you ... and his survival depends on you.

That's the formula. It works in the Parachute Regiment. It works in the Maasai Mara. And it works for those of us navigating the daily battlefield of anxiety.

MEANWHILE, BACK IN MODERN BRITAIN ...

Right. So that's how humans organised themselves successfully for millennia, and how I experienced it personally in uniform.

Back in modern life, we've invented open-plan offices, self-checkout machines and the phrase: 'Sorry, I'm just really busy at the moment.'

We've become extraordinarily good at being alone – together.

We sit in trains packed with people, faces buried in phones, avoiding eye contact as if acknowledging another human might demand ... commitment. We live in blocks of flats where we don't know our neighbours' names. We've replaced community with connectivity and then we wonder why we feel so profoundly disconnected.

The average British adult has fewer close friends than at any point in recorded history. We're told to be self-sufficient, resilient, independent.

'You've got this,' we tell each other. Translation: 'Please don't make your problems my problems.'

And into this isolation slips anxiety, whispering its familiar lies: 'You're the only one. Nobody else struggles like this. You're fundamentally broken in a way nobody could understand.'

It's absolute bollocks.

THE 'ANXIETY TRIBE'

Here's why I use the word tribe throughout this book. It's not a trend. It carries weight, history and a profound truth about how humans function. And it's because I've lived it. I know what it feels like to be part of a tribe that would die for each other. I know the strength of shared purpose. I know that bonds forged under pressure are the ones that last.

If you have anxiety – real, keeps-you-awake-at-night, makes-your-palms-sweat-before-meetings, turns-your-stomach-into-a-washing-machine anxiety – you are not alone.

You are part of a massive, sprawling, global tribe of people who know exactly what you mean when you describe that feeling: the hard-to-explain sense that something is terribly wrong, even when nothing is actually wrong.

SOMEWHERE, RIGHT NOW, AS YOU READ THIS:

- Someone in Tokyo is lying awake with the same racing thoughts.
- Someone in São Paulo is catastrophising about their work presentation.
- Someone in Edinburgh is convinced that their perfectly normal headache is actually a brain tumour.
- And ... somewhere in a farmhouse in rural England, someone is having a cup of tea and worrying about all the ways this book might fail.

That last one? That's me, obviously.

The Anxiety Tribe isn't something I invented. It already existed. I'm just giving it a name – and a flag to rally around. I might even give it a dodgy logo one day if the branding budget allows.

CHAPTER TWO

WHY TRIBALISM WORKS (EVEN FOR US ANXIOUS LOT)

The Maasai can spot another Maasai from miles away – from the shuka, the beadwork, the walk. There's an instant recognition, an unspoken realisation: one of mine.

1. RECOGNITION

In the Paras, it was the same. You could see it in the way a bloke carried himself – the slight swagger, the directness, the complete absence of bullshit. You could spot a fellow Para in a crowded room within seconds, even out of uniform.

The Anxiety Tribe has its own markers too. **They include:**

- The slightly nervous laugh after saying something completely normal
- The reflexive apologising
- The thousand-yard stare when someone asks, 'Are you okay?'

The way we detect another anxious person across a crowded room is like some kind of broken radar system. It shouldn't work, but it does. When you meet another tribe member, something clicks. You don't have to explain yourself because they already know.

That recognition – that instant 'me too' – is profoundly healing.

2. SHARED LANGUAGE

Every tribe develops its own vocabulary.

The Inuit famously have multiple words for snow. Paratroopers have an entire dictionary civilians wouldn't understand (and probably shouldn't). And the Anxiety Tribe has multiple words for the precise flavour of dread you feel when your phone rings unexpectedly.

We understand 'spiralling', 'catastrophising', 'doom scrolling' and 'anxiety poo' (don't pretend you don't know what I'm talking about). We know the difference between 'a bit worried' and 'utterly convinced the world is ending and it's probably my fault.' We speak the same language of distress.

This matters. When you don't have to translate your experience –when someone just gets it – the isolation dissolves. You're no longer trapped in your own head. You're communicating with your people.

3. COLLECTIVE RESILIENCE

A single Zulu warrior is impressive. Ten thousand Zulu warriors at Isandlwana rewrote British military history.

A single Para is dangerous. A battalion of Paras took Goose Green against odds that should have been impossible.

An individual anxiety sufferer is vulnerable. We question our own perceptions, assume our experience isn't valid because nobody talks about it, suffer in silence, and mistake that silence for normality.

But the Anxiety Tribe?

We are millions strong. We are not vulnerable. We are a force.

When we share our stories, we normalise the experience. When we support each other, we prove that anxiety isn't a personal failing but a human one. And when we stand together and say, 'Yes, this is real, and no, you're not mad,' we don't just comfort each other, we change the conversation.

4. THE POWER OF 'ME TOO'

The San Bushmen don't hunt alone – they track together, following the same antelope, sharing the same hardships and celebrating the same kill.

There's something almost magical about hearing another human say, 'That happens to me too.' They're not offering advice or solutions – just recognition.

When someone describes their anxiety and I nod and

say, 'Yeah, I get that', I'm not being dismissive.

I'm doing the most powerful thing one tribe member can do for another ... confirming that their experience is real, valid and shared. You're not uniquely broken – you're normally broken, just like the rest of us.

Welcome ... the kettle's on.

5. PERMISSION TO NOT BE FINE

Modern life demands that we are always 'fine'.

- 'How are you?'

Fine.

- 'How's work?'

Fine.

- 'How's your mental health?'

Fine, thanks, fine.

Please, don't ask follow-up questions – I'm British.

The Anxiety Tribe gives you permission to not be fine. We're not fine and probably haven't been for years. And that's okay. More than okay – it's honest.

When you're surrounded by people who know that 'fine' is usually a lie, you can finally stop lying. You can say, 'Actually, I'm having a terrible day. My anxiety is through the roof, and I've convinced myself everyone secretly hates me.'

And someone will say, 'God, same. Want to talk about it?'

That's a tribe. That's the whole point.

6. FORGED UNDER PRESSURE

The military taught me something that applies directly to the Anxiety Tribe: the strongest bonds are formed under the worst conditions.

Nobody becomes a Para because it's easy. You become a Para because you survived P Company alongside other men who survived P Company. You share something that can't be explained to anyone who wasn't there. The suffering becomes a badge of honour, a shared history and an unbreakable connection.

Anxiety is our P Company.

I'm not being flippant. Living with genuine anxiety is hard, exhausting, and a daily battle most people can't see – and therefore assume doesn't exist. But everyone who fights that battle shares something profound. We've been through it. We're still going through it. That shared struggle creates bonds that comfortable people will never understand.

The tribe isn't strong despite the hardship, it's strong because of it.

7. INHERITED WISDOM

The Himba pass down essential knowledge through generations –where to find water, which plants heal and which can kill.

The Anxiety Tribe has its own version of inherited wisdom: accumulated techniques, coping strategies and approaches that actually work. It's the collective knowledge of millions who've been exactly where you are and found a way through.

You don't have to figure it out from scratch. The tribe has already left trail markers, mapped the pitfalls and documented what works. You only need to be willing to listen.

8. RITUALS AND PRACTICES

Every tribe has rituals. The Maasai have the jumping dance; the Zulu the reed ceremony and the San perform healing dances around the fire.

The Anxiety Tribe has rituals too, even if they look different:

- Breathing exercises
- Grounding techniques
- Morning routines that keep us stable
- Evening walks that quiet the mind

The shared language we use to check in: 'How's the anxiety today?' 'Manageable. Yours?' 'Bit spicy.'

Rituals create rhythm. They remind us that we are part of something larger than our individual panic.

9. A PLACE TO BELONG

This is the big one – the reason tribes exist at all. Humans need to belong; it's wired into us at a genetic level.

Historically, being excluded from the tribe meant death. Your brain still thinks that's true, which is why rejection hurts like physical pain and why isolation can drive us mad.

The Anxiety Tribe offers what our fragmented, individualistic, 'you've got this' society does not: genuine belonging. Not because you've achieved something or proved yourself worthy, but simply because you are here. You are one of us … and that is enough.

CHAPTER THREE

YOU'RE REALLY NOT ALONE

Here's what I need you to understand—and I don't mean just nod, intellectually acknowledge it and forget—really understand.

Right now, as you read this, thousands of people are feeling anxiety. The same racing heart. The same churning stomach. The same catastrophic thoughts. They're scattered across the globe, yet experiencing the exact same human reality.

THEY ARE YOUR TRIBE:

- High-powered executives pretending they're fine in board meetings.
- University students lying awake at 2 am, heart pounding.
- Parents hiding in the bathroom for five precious minutes of peace.
- Soldiers who've faced combat and now can't even face Tesco without a plan.

They're all your people. And here's the kicker, they all think they're alone too. Every single one of them secretly believes their anxiety is shameful, weak, proof that they're fundamentally broken.

They're wrong. You're wrong. We're all wrong … together.

And that, perhaps, is the most tribe-like thing of all.

A TRIBE ISN'T WHAT YOU THINK IT IS

Let me be clear about something because this matters.

Being part of a tribe has nothing to do with where you come from.

Nothing to do with your postcode, your passport, your parents, your pigmentation or your politics.

Those are accidents of birth. Demographics. Admin.

A tribe is forged.

Built.

Earned.

It's formed through shared experience and common purpose.

I served alongside men from every conceivable background: Welsh farmers, London lads, Scottish Highlanders, blokes from Birmingham and Belfast and everywhere in between. Different accents. Different upbringings. Different views on everything from football to foreign policy.

None of that mattered. Not a bit of it.

What mattered was whether you could trust the man next to you when things went sideways.

What mattered was shared commitment to a common goal. What mattered was the unspoken understanding that we were all in this together and nobody was getting left behind.

That's a tribe.

The rest is just demographics.

The Anxiety Tribe works the same way.

We come from every background imaginable – rich, poor, educated, unschooled, young, old, every colour, creed and orientation you can think of. We're not united by how we look or where we're from, but by what we share: this peculiar, often paralysing experience of living with anxiety.

That shared experience makes us stronger together than we could ever be alone.

This isn't about sympathy or pity or handholding. It's about a practical truth: a group of people with a common goal, forged under pressure, supporting each other through difficulty, will always outperform a collection of isolated individuals.

The military proved that to me.

Life has proved it again since.

AN INVITATION

So here's my invitation – and I don't extend it lightly.

Join the tribe.

Not just as a reader of this book, but as an active, card-carrying (okay, there aren't cards ... yet) member of the Anxiety Tribe. Claim your membership. Stop pretending you're fine when you're not. Start talking about this stuff with people you trust.

Find your fellow tribe members.

They're everywhere ... hiding in plain sight, waiting for someone else to go first.

When you meet another anxious person, nod in recognition. You're one of mine.

When you see someone struggling, offer the words they need to hear: 'Me too.'

When you're struggling yourself, remember this: you are not alone.

You're part of something ancient, powerful and deeply fundamentally human.

The Maasai say, 'The child who is not embraced by the village will burn it down to feel its warmth.'

You don't need to burn anything down.

The warmth is already there, waiting for you.

All you have to do is stop pretending you don't need it and come home to your tribe.

Welcome to the Anxiety Tribe, my friend.

We've saved you a seat.

It's slightly uncomfortable, and someone's probably anxious about whether you'll like it, but it's yours.

You belong here.

You always did.

CHAPTER FOUR

THE NIGHT IT ALL BEGAN (IT WAS 2 AM ... OBVIOUSLY.)

Anxiety doesn't knock politely. It doesn't send an email saying, 'Hello, I'd like to schedule some existential dread for next Tuesday at 3 pm, if that works for your calendar.'

No. Anxiety is that mate who shows up drunk at your door at closing time, demanding to be let in.

I was forty-one. Spent years in the army, countless jumps from planes, bullets dodged, companies built, failure, successful, wins and wins and the odd loses – and there I was, lying in bed, absolutely certain I was about to die.

My heart was playing a drum solo at a metal concert, my chest felt like it had been clamped in a vice, my arms tingled and my brain –my brilliant, rational brain that had guided me through firefights –had decided the only logical explanation was imminent cardiac arrest.

So, naturally, I did what any sensible man would: I lay

perfectly still, monitoring my own heartbeat, waiting for death.

It didn't come.

What did come was the same thing the next night. And the night after that. And the night after that.

Welcome to anxiety, you poor bastard.

NOT A RANDOM AMBUSH

Let me take you back a bit further, because that first night wasn't a random ambush. It had been building for a while, like a storm sitting on the horizon pretending it wasn't coming.

I'd been pushing hard in business – closing deals with multiple zeros, bouncing between London and Europe like a human yo-yo, permanently jet-lagged and running on caffeine and adrenaline. I ignored the early warning signs: the occasional skipped heartbeat during a board meeting, the constant tightness in my jaw that I brushed off as 'stress'.

Stress was for civilians.

I was Adam Knights—paratrooper turned entrepreneur. I ate stress for breakfast.

Then came the night in question. I was home alone, my wife out with friends, and I'd just polished off a late-night curry that probably didn't help. But honestly, it wasn't the spice – it was the silence. In the Paras, silence meant danger. And here, in my posh suburban bedroom, it meant my mind had free rein to invent horrors.

That heart palpitation?

Not indigestion.

No, sir.

That was the Grim Reaper sharpening his scythe.

I rolled over, grabbed my phone, and typed 'heart attack symptoms' into Google. A catastrophic decision. The screen lit up with a list that matched me perfectly – arm tingling? Check. Chest pain? Double check.

I sat bolt upright, sweating like I'd just run a marathon, and rang my mate Mark, a fellow ex-Para.

'Mark,' I whispered, 'I think this is it.'

He laughed. He told me to drink some water and go back to bed. 'You're not dying, you knob. You're just old.'

He was right.

But that didn't stop the cycle.

The next week, it hit again – this time during a client dinner. Halfway through dessert, my vision blurred. I excused myself, locked myself in the loo, splashed water on my face and stared at my reflection like it had betrayed me.

'Pull yourself together,' I muttered.

It only made the knot tighter.

Looking back, that first night was my introduction to anxiety's dark humour. It can turn a tough bloke into a hypochondriac faster than you can Google it. And the irony? I'd dodged real bullets in Belfast, only to find myself dodging imaginary ones in my own bedroom.

CHAPTER FIVE

FIGHTING THE INVISIBLE ENEMY

'The more I tried to suppress the panic, the more panicked I became about being panicked. It's a beautifully recursive nightmare.'– Adam Knights

Here's what the Parachute Regiment teaches you: when you encounter an enemy, you close with and destroy them –violence of action, aggression, speed.

So when anxiety showed up, I did exactly that.

I went to war.

I researched. I strategised. I threw money at the problem. I met therapists, swallowed supplements, downloaded meditation apps and read books with titles like *Conquer Your Anxiety*, *Defeat Your Fear* and *Absolutely Annihilate Your Nervous System's Perfectly Natural Responses*.

And what happened?

The anxiety got worse.

Every time I fought it, it came back stronger. The harder I pushed, the more stuck I became. The more I tried to suppress the panic, the more panicked I felt about being panicked.

Anxiety is a beautifully recursive nightmare. Elegant, in its own twisted way, which you'll appreciate fully … at 2 am. Every night.

I was locked in combat with an enemy that fed on combat. It took me years to realise I was using the wrong tactics entirely.

ANXIETY SKIRMISHES

1. A high-stakes healthcare acquisition

The room was full of suits. Spreadsheets everywhere. And then – my hands went numb. Not a mild tingle. Full-on 'are these even attached?' numb.

In the Paras, numbness meant frostbite or worse. But here?

I excused myself, popped a beta-blocker I'd sourced from somewhere I won't name (don't judge … desperation is a hell of a drug) and went back in telling myself to fight through it.

The numbness spread to my face.

I torpedoed the deal by blurting out nonsense about 'synergistic paradigms', while internally screaming.

That night I launched a full assault: gym session until collapse, ice-cold shower, then a horror film to 'toughen up'.

Result? A panic attack that was so severe I ended up in A&E, convinced I was having a stroke.

The doctor glanced at my chart and said,

'Anxiety, mate. Take it easy.'

Easy?

I'd rather take a bullet.

2. The meditation retreat

I signed up for a week in the Welsh countryside, convinced that silence would starve the beast.

- **Day one:** Fine.
- **Day two:** The quiet turned hostile. What if I never sell another company? What if my wife leaves because I'm a wreck?
- **Day three:** I was hiding in my room, breathing into a paper bag.

The guru said, 'Embrace the void'.

So I embraced the void with single malt and zopiclone.

Dark humour alert: anxiety took me from Rambo to a man who cries at dog videos. I'd laugh now if it wasn't so painfully accurate. But those fights taught me something important – aggression against your own brain is like nuking your own backyard.

The Elephant in the Room

(How I learned to tell death to politely piss off)

Right. Let's talk about the thing nobody wants to talk about.

If you've picked up this book, there's a decent chance you've stood at that crossroads – the one where anxiety has dragged you so far into the dark that the idea of an exit starts to look tempting. Not because you want to disappear, but because you want the noise, the pressure, the relentless suffocation to stop.

I'm not going to pretend I haven't been there. I have. More than once. And if you're honest with yourself, there's a good chance you have too.

So let's stop pretending the elephant isn't in the room. Pull up a chair. Make him a cup of tea. Ignoring him hasn't worked for anyone yet.

Here's what I've learned: anxiety and thoughts of escape are far more closely linked than polite conversation ever admits.

When your brain has been shouting catastrophe at you for hours or days, when sleep has become a rumour and your body feels permanently braced for impact, the idea of making it all stop can start to sound … reasonable.

Not romantic. Not poetic. Just persuasive.

It's like a salesman who's caught you at your absolute lowest and knows exactly when to pitch. 'I can make this end,' he whispers. 'Right now.'

And in that moment, all the well-meaning things you've been told – about guilt, about loved ones, about how it gets better – can sound like complete nonsense. Because when you're that deep in it, you don't feel like a person with a future. You feel like a problem that needs solving.

You don't worry about leaving people behind because your anxiety has already convinced you they'd be better off. You don't feel guilt, because guilt requires a sense of worth, and anxiety has spent the last few days dismantling that belief piece by piece.

The idea that things might improve feels as plausible as winning the lottery while being struck by lightning on a Tuesday.

I'm not saying this to be grim. I'm saying it so that if you've been there, you understand this: you're not broken. You're not uniquely weak. You're not the one person in history whose dark thoughts mean something terrible about who you are.

You're human. And your nervous system is exhausted and looking – desperately – for a way out of pain that feels endless.

So what do you do when that salesman comes knocking?

I'm not a doctor or a therapist, and I'm not pretending this is universal advice. But I can tell you what's worked for me.

I don't argue with the thought. I don't try to out-logic it. Logic packed up and left a few breakdowns ago. And I don't pretend the thought isn't there.

I just say: 'Not today. Thank you. Please call back another time.'

That's it. That's the whole strategy.

Not forever. Just for now.

THE THERAPY SHOPPING LIST (HOW I GOT BANNED FROM SUNBATHING AT THE PRIORY)

I've tried a lot of things over the years.

Some helped. Some didn't.

A few made things actively worse.

Let's start with The Priory. Yes, that Priory – the one celebrities disappear into when their publicist says they're 'taking time out'.

I checked myself in after a particularly spectacular spiral, convinced that proper professional help, in a proper professional setting, would finally fix me.

There were group sessions with people whose stories made my own feel almost quaint, and there were industrial quantities of Cognitive Behavioural Therapy (CBT) – the darling of the mental-health world.

But the real highlight came on a rare British midsummer afternoon. One of those days when the sun turns up like it actually means it. I was sitting in the beautiful, tranquil garden and thought, Why not catch a few rays on the old body? So I took my top off.

Within minutes, a member of staff materialised beside me and very politely asked me to put my T-shirt back on.

'We do have sex addicts here as well,' she explained, in the calm, practised tone of someone who's had this conversation before.

I looked at her.

She looked at me.

A beat passed.

'What room is she in?' I asked.

She didn't laugh. Not even a flicker. Just stone-faced professionalism. I put my T-shirt back on.

The Priory wasn't for me.

And neither was CBT.

That didn't mean therapy wasn't for me – it just meant I had to keep shopping.

And this is the bit I want you to take away: don't give up on therapy just because the first thing you try doesn't work. CBT might be your thing. Psychoanalysis might be your thing. So might EMDR, hypnotherapy or something else entirely.

The point is that something will click.

Find your combination. Build your toolkit. Mix and match until you've got something that keeps you functional, keeps you moving and most importantly, keeps you here.

That's all any of us are really trying to do … stay here, keep going and occasionally, on sunny days, take our T-shirts off in inappropriate places.

They still haven't told me what room she was in.

PART TWO

THE SURRENDER

(How I stopped punching myself and tried hugging instead)

CHAPTER SIX

LEARNING TO SAY HELLO TO MY ANXIETY

'Say hello to your anxiety. Not to banish it, but to acknowledge it. Because what we face, we can handle. What we ignore, handles us.'– Adam Knights

The first step in any relationship is acknowledgement. You can't love someone you're pretending doesn't exist.

That sounds obvious when we're talking about humans. You don't build a friendship by crossing the street every time you see someone. Yet that's exactly what most of us do with anxiety. We pretend it isn't there, hoping that if we ignore it hard enough, it'll get bored and wander off to terrorise someone else.

Spoiler alert: it doesn't.

TALKING TO MY ANXIETY

So I started talking to my anxiety – sometimes out loud, which probably concerned my neighbour. My neighbour thinks I've lost the plot. I once caught her peering through her net curtains while I was having a full conversation with my chest in the garden.

I can't really blame her. There I was – a fifty-two-year-old former Para – standing by my begonias at 7 am, saying, 'Morning, you absolute bastard. You're here early,' to apparently nothing. I did the same thing when I woke up first thing in the morning too.

It sounded mad, and it felt mad. The first few times I did it, I half expected men in white coats to abseil through my bedroom window. But something interesting happened: the anxiety didn't like being noticed. It preferred operating in the shadows, building up steam while I pretended everything was fine. When I acknowledged it directly, it seemed almost ... embarrassed.

It was like catching your teenage daughter sneaking in at 2 am. The stealth mission was compromised.

In the Parachute Regiment, we had a saying: acknowledge the threat before it acknowledges you. Usually, that meant noticing the bloke with an AK-47 before he noticed you, which is admittedly more life-or-death than saying hello to your feelings. Still, the principle transfers remarkably well.

Anxiety is a sneaky little operator. It prefers the element of surprise. It creeps up when you're not paying attention – whether you're in the shower, halfway through a meeting, or at 3 am just as you've drifted off to sleep.

But here's the thing about sneaky operators: they rely on you not looking. The moment you turn around and say, 'I see you, mate', their entire strategy falls apart.

It's the military equivalent of shining a torch into a dark corner. Whatever was lurking there suddenly looks a lot less terrifying once you can actually see it. Nine times out of ten, the monster in the shadows turns out to be a mop.

Unfortunately, my anxiety wasn't a mop. It was more like a pink spaghetti ball with googly eyes and an attitude problem. Still, she became far less intimidating once I started acknowledging her presence.

Let me give you a personal example from my early 'hello' phase.

I was in a boardroom, pitching investors on my latest venture – a health tech app, ironically. Slide seven of twelve. I was explaining market penetration strategies to a room full of suits who could smell fear like sharks smell blood. And mid-sentence – right between 'synergistic' and 'value proposition' (words I hate but was using anyway), the chest tightness hit like a vice.

The old me would have panicked, felt the squeeze, catastrophised about having a heart attack in front of potential investors, started sweating, forgotten my own name and probably excused myself to have a breakdown in the toilets while the deal evaporated along with my dignity.

The new me just paused, took a sip of water and whispered under my breath,

'Hello, mate. Joining the pitch, are we?'

The investors didn't hear a thing. They just assumed

I was taking a deliberate pause, building tension before hitting them with the big numbers. Little did they know I was having a quiet conversation with my neurotic co-pilot.

And here's the thing ... it worked.

Not perfectly. The anxiety didn't disappear in a puff of smoke. But it did back off, just enough. It retreated to a manageable hum instead of a deafening roar, and I nailed the rest of the pitch. We got the funding. I celebrated with a pint, toasting my invisible companion.

'Cheers, you pink bitch. We make a good team.'

The investor story sounds dramatic, but the technique works just as well in far more mundane situations – sometimes better, because the mundane ones catch you off guard.

Take grocery shopping ...

I was in Tesco, aisle five, minding my own business among the cereals, when dread washed over me. No reason. Just because.

This is one of anxiety's favourite tricks – striking when absolutely nothing threatening is happening, just to remind you who's boss. There I was, wedged between the Weetabix and the Coco Pops, heart racing, palms sweating, convinced something terrible was about to happen.

What terrible thing? Who knows. That's not anxiety's department. Anxiety just slams the alarm button and leaves you to work out why the building's on fire. Of course, the building wasn't on fire. It was a perfectly normal Tesco at 2 pm on a Tuesday.

I stopped, picked up a box of Weetabix, and said out loud, 'Alright, anxiety? Fancy some breakfast?'

A woman with a trolley full of cat food looked at me like I'd just announced I was the reincarnation of Napoleon. Fair enough. I probably did look completely unhinged, chatting to breakfast cereals in the middle of a supermarket. But here's what I've learned: you can either look sane and feel insane or look slightly odd and feel relatively okay.

I'll take the latter.

The dread deflated like a punctured balloon. Not completely – anxiety doesn't vanish that easily – but enough. Enough to finish my shopping. Enough to drive home without pulling over. Enough to get on with my day.

The cat food woman probably still tells people about the time she saw a madman proposing to breakfast cereals. I hope I brightened her day.

Anxiety is a bit like a cat. It wants attention when it wants attention, but the moment you acknowledge it properly, it gets uncomfortable and wanders off to lick itself in a corner.

Think about it. Cats spend all day demanding food, affection and access to the one room in the house you've deliberately closed off. But the second you sit down and give them your full, undivided attention, they look at you like you've committed a war crime and stalk off as if to say,

'How dare you look at me. I was trying to manipulate you from the shadows.'

Anxiety operates in much the same way. It builds in the background, getting louder and more insistent, feeding on your attempts to ignore it – rather like a toddler throwing a tantrum.

The more you pretend nothing's happening, the more committed the toddler becomes to ensuring you fully grasp the injustice of not being allowed a third ice cream. But if you turn and face the toddler, the cat or the anxiety, they suddenly don't know what to do with themselves. You've broken the spell. You've refused to play the game.

'Oh,' your anxiety seems to say, caught in the act. 'You can see me? Well ... this is awkward.'

And then it skulks off to regroup, probably plotting its next ambush – but at least you've bought yourself some breathing room.

I should be honest here: the hello technique doesn't always work perfectly. Sometimes you say hello and anxiety waves back cheerfully and settles in for a long visit, like an in-law who's brought a suitcase. Other times, you acknowledge it and it gets louder, offended that you're not taking it seriously enough.

There was one night I'll never forget. I woke at 2 am, with the familiar grip in my chest and thought, Right. I know what to do now. Hello, anxiety.

But instead of backing off, my pink spaghetti mistress pulled up a chair, cracked open a beer and said,

'Oh good, you're awake. I've got so much to tell you.'

She spent the next three hours cataloguing every decision I'd ever made, every relationship I'd ever botched and every professional email I'd ever sent that might have come across as even slightly passive-aggressive. By 5 am, we'd covered my entire life history and were well into speculative future disasters that hadn't even happened yet.

'You know what's going to happen when you die?' she asked cheerfully. 'Your kids will find your browser history.'

Thanks for that.

But here's the thing ... even that night was better than the alternative. Before I learned to say hello, that 2 am ambush would have sent me spiralling. I would have fought it, panicked about panicking, convinced myself I was having a breakdown and probably ended up in A&E asking doctors to check whether there was something physically wrong with my heart. The war would have lasted days, not hours.

Instead, I had a long, annoying night with an unwelcome house guest, and then she left. Not forever – because she never leaves forever – but she did leave.

Sometimes that's all you can ask for.

I've tried the hello technique in all sorts of situations since then, with varying degrees of success and public embarrassment:

- **On planes:** 'Hello, old chap. Turbulence, is it?' (The man next to me asked if I was okay. I told him I was talking to my feelings. He asked to change seats.)
- **In traffic:** 'Welcome aboard, love. Yes, the M25

is a nightmare. No, I probably won't die today.' (Someone in the next lane gave me a thumbs up. Either solidarity, or they thought I was on hands-free.)

- **During important phone calls:** 'Ah, there you are. Going to make my voice shake, are we? Crack on then.' (My boss asked who I was talking to. I said, 'Quality control.' I don't know what that means either.)
- **Even, on one memorably awkward occasion, during sex.** I don't recommend this one.

The key to the hello technique – and this took me months to understand – is that you're not trying to make the anxiety go away. You're not saying hello as a magic spell to banish it. You're saying hello as a way of changing your relationship with it.

When I was fighting anxiety, it was the enemy – an invader, something to be destroyed. And you know what? It didn't work. Because you can't destroy your own nervous system, and you can't defeat a part of yourself in combat. That's like trying to win a fight against your own left arm. Even if you somehow manage it, you've still lost.

But when you say hello, everything shifts. You're not fighting anymore. You're acknowledging, noticing, making space. It's the difference between 'GET OUT OF MY HEAD' and 'Oh, you're here again. Alright then.' One is a declaration of war. The other is a shrug.

And here's the thing about wars: they escalate. The more you fight, the more you have to fight. Your anxiety responds to resistance by turning up the volume, sending reinforcements and deploying new weapons.

Before you know it, you're not just anxious – you're anxious about being anxious, terrified of the terror, panicking about the panic. It's a feedback loop straight to hell.

But a shrug? A shrug doesn't escalate. A shrug says, 'I see you. I hear you. I'm not impressed.'

That's surprisingly powerful.

Try it now. Seriously. Don't just read this – do it. Next time you feel that creeping dread, don't push it away. Don't pretend it isn't there. Don't grit your teeth, soldier on, and tell yourself to stop being ridiculous.

Look at it and say hello.

'Oh, there you are. Wondered when you'd show up.'

You can say it out loud if you want. You can say it in your head. You can say it in a silly voice, a stern voice or a bored voice. The exact words don't matter. What matters is the acknowledgement, the turning to face it and the refusal to pretend.

Here are my personal favourites, developed over two years of practise:

'Top of the morning, you absolute nightmare.'

'Fancy meeting you here. How long are you staying?'

'Right, you're here. Noted. Moving on.'

'Hello again, my pink spaghetti mistress. What fresh

hell have you got planned?'

The dark humour works because laughing at your own terror takes the edge off. Anxiety hates it. It wants to be taken seriously, and it wants you to believe that this time, it really is something to worry about.

Saying, 'Hello, you ridiculous pink gorgeous thing', is a way of calling its bluff.

I'm not going to pretend this is easy. It took weeks to get past the feeling that I was losing my mind every time I talked to my own feelings. It took months to make it a habit, and years to make it automatic.

And it doesn't cure anything. Anxiety still shows up – ambushing me in supermarkets and boardrooms, at 3 am when I'm trying to sleep. The difference is that now we know each other. There's a relationship. Instead of two enemies locked in combat, we're more like reluctant flatmates sharing a space. She still leaves her dishes in the sink; I still wish she'd move out. But we manage.

The hello is just the beginning – the first date, the opening handshake. It's the moment you stop pretending this thing doesn't exist and start figuring out how to live with it. Here's a truth nobody likes to hear: your anxiety isn't going anywhere. You can't defeat it, cure it, or meditate, medicate or exercise it out of existence. It's part of you – maybe the most persistent, annoying, unwelcome part – but part of you, nonetheless.

The only question is: what kind of relationship do you

want to have with it? War? Been there, tried that and lost badly. Or maybe … something else that starts with a simple hello.

Mrs Patterson from number forty-two might think I'm barking mad. But she hasn't slept through the night in thirty years because she's too busy fighting her own demons instead of inviting them in for tea.

Trust me … say hello. It's the sanest thing you'll ever do.

CHAPTER SEVEN

WHY MY ANXIETY IS FEMALE AND WHY I TOOK HER OUT TO BREAKFAST

'Anxiety is a pink spaghetti monster with googly eyes and an attitude problem ... and she's mine.' – Adam Knights

THE FIRST DATE

After more than twenty-five years of fighting, I decided to try something different: I asked my anxiety out on a date.

I know how that sounds – trust me, I know. But hear me out ... I'd spent over two decades trying to defeat this thing: silencing it, medicating it, drinking it into submission. None of it worked. The anxiety just kept showing up, like the world's most persistent ex who refuses to accept that the relationship is over. So I reasoned: if I couldn't get rid of it, maybe I should try getting along with it.

At first, I thought coffee would work. Quick, casual, low commitment. But then I reconsidered – coffee felt too rushed. If I was genuinely going to try building a relationship with the thing that had been ruining my life, I needed to invest more than the price of a flat white. So I booked a table for two at a proper breakfast place: tablecloths, good eggs, the works.

The waiter gave me a look when I confirmed it was a table for two, then seated me alone. I could see him scanning the restaurant for my companion. When nobody appeared, he placed the second menu down anyway, professional to the last.

'Your guest will be joining you shortly?' he asked.

'She's already here,' I said, gesturing to the empty chair. 'She's just invisible.'

He blinked, nodded slowly and backed away with the careful movements of someone who had decided not to make any sudden gestures.

We talked for two hours. Properly talked. It wasn't the usual screaming match – her telling me I'm dying, me telling her to shut up. It was a real conversation. She told me about the times she'd saved my life, the near-misses I'd avoided because she made me paranoid enough to check twice. I told her about the times she'd nearly destroyed me – the opportunities I'd missed because I was too scared to take them, the relationships I'd sabotaged.

We both had valid points, and that was the uncomfortable truth. We'd both been doing our best, and we'd both made a complete mess of it.

By the time the waiter came to clear the plates, I knew what I had to do. I said to her, 'I love you.'

WHY MY ANXIETY IS FEMALE

Before we go any further, I need to address something that might have half of you reaching for your keyboards to fire off an angry email, and that is this: my anxiety is female. Not because I have issues with women, but because the creature that first planted this seed in my chest wore a tweed skirt and smelled of disappointment.

It was the 1970s. I was five years old, attending a primary school that operated under educational principles best described as Victorian, with occasional violence. My teacher – let's call her Mrs Chambers, because that wasn't her name but she's probably dead now and I'd rather not have her ghost haunting me on top of everything else – viewed children the way a particularly stern farmer views livestock. We were useful occasionally, tolerable rarely, and always in need of regular correction.

Mrs Chambers had a gift, and it was not for teaching. God, no. Her gift was identifying weakness with the precision of a sniper scope. And my weakness? My brain's absolute refusal to make letters sit still on a page.

We call it dyslexia now, but back then they called it 'not trying hard enough', 'being deliberately difficult' or my personal favourite, 'the boy doesn't listen'.

The educational establishment of 1970s' Britain had a very sophisticated diagnostic framework for learning difficulties, which went as follows: if the child couldn't do it, the child was either stupid or lazy. Treatment options were equally advanced and consisted of a sharp word, public humiliation, or – if things got clinical – a good hard smack, followed eventually by exile to the woodwork shed.

I couldn't write my own name. Not properly, and certainly not the way the other kids could. The letters would jumble and twist, staging their own little rebellion against whatever my hand was trying to do. To Mrs Chambers, this wasn't a neurological difference. It was insubordination.

Picture the scene …

Thirty children sit in rows, the smell of poster paint and fear hanging in the air. And me: a small, confused kid who desperately wanted to please, staring at a page where 'Adam' had somehow become 'Adma' or 'Aadm' or occasionally just a sort of hopeful squiggle.

'Come here, boy.'

Those three words, even now, fortyodd years later, land in my stomach like concrete. The walk to her desk was about twelve feet, but it felt like twelve miles, each step accompanied by the delighted terror of my classmates, who were just grateful it wasn't them.

Mrs Chambers sat behind her desk like a magistrate – if magistrates wore reading glasses on chains and had the emotional warmth of a frozen fish finger.

'What is this?'

She held up my work, not to me but to the class. Evidence for the prosecution.

I'd mumble something. I don't remember what, and it

didn't matter. Nothing I said mattered. The verdict was already in.

And then I received the correction. The educational intervention. The considered, pedagogically sound response to a child with a processing disorder.

Whack.

Being hit as a child for something your brain physically cannot do does not improve your spelling. What it does do, with remarkable efficiency, is install a passenger – a voice, a presence – that will ride shotgun in your skull for the next several decades, waiting patiently to whisper that you're stupid, you're wrong and you're about to be found out.

That presence, in my head, has always been female. She sounds like Mrs Chambers, dresses like Mrs Chambers and sighs before she speaks, as if the very act of addressing me is exhausting her.

I didn't know it then, but Mrs Chambers was building something in me. And it wasn't confidence, or education, or a love of learning. She was steadily laying the foundations of an anxiety disorder that would take up residence in my chest for the next five decades. And she made it in her own image.

To be fair to Mrs Chambers, she was a product of her time. Teachers in the 1970s weren't trained to spot dyslexia; they were trained to produce neat handwriting and compliant children. She probably went home each night genuinely believing she was doing her job. Perhaps she had a cat. Perhaps she did needlepoint. Perhaps she was perfectly lovely outside that classroom, full of warmth and kindness and gentle humanity.

I doubt it, but perhaps.

What I know for certain is that somewhere between the ages of five and seven, I learned that I was fundamentally wrong. Not wrong in a way that could be corrected with practice or patience, but wrong in a way that invited punishment. Wrong in a way that needed to be hidden.

And the part of me that learned that lesson? She's still with me. She grew up alongside me, fed on every failure, every embarrassment, every moment where I felt out of my depth. She learned new words as I learned them, graduated from 'stupid boy' to 'incompetent' to 'fraud'. As my vocabulary expanded, she adapted. She evolved.

She became sophisticated.

But here's the thing they don't tell you about the monsters built in childhood: they're yours. Mrs Chambers may have planted the seed and watered it with fear and shame, but the thing that grew? She's mine. And once I understood that this anxious, critical, endlessly vigilant presence wasn't some external curse, but a part of me that had been trying – clumsily, obsessively and sometimes destructively – to keep me safe all along, everything started to change.

But I'm getting ahead of myself.

Before we can fall in love with our anxiety, we need

to understand why she's such an absolute nightmare of a house guest. And for that, we need to go back to that classroom one more time. Not to blame Mrs Chambers. Not to exorcise her ghost. But, oddly enough, to thank her.

Because without her, I might never have met the most infuriating, most persistent and ultimately most valuable relationship of my life: my pink spaghetti mistress.

GIVE YOUR ANXIETY A FACE

(and how to make friends with your pink spaghetti monster)

Here's something that sounds completely mad but actually works, give your anxiety a face. A name. A colour. A sex. A personality. Make it something.

Because right now, your anxiety is probably a vast, formless, omnipotent force that controls everything. It's everywhere and nowhere at once and fighting it feels like trying to punch the weather.

And the thing about formless, omnipotent forces is that they're terrifying.

You know what's less terrifying?

A pink spaghetti ball with googly eyes.

That's mine. A tangled, messy pink spaghetti ball. She has enormous eyes that never stop watching and a big mouth that never stops talking. She's sitting with me now, perched on my shoulder as I type this. She's probably checking my spelling – because I'm dyslexic –and therefore she has plenty of material to work with.

This is our relationship now.

She still makes her little comments. The same kinds of comments teachers in the 1970s used to make about boys like me. That we're stupid. Thick. Never going anywhere.

But instead of crumbling – instead of believing every word – I can look at this ridiculous pink spaghetti creature and think: Oh. It's just you again.

That's the magic of giving anxiety a form: you separate it from yourself.

When anxiety is formless, it feels like you. The thoughts feel like your thoughts. The cruel internal monologue sounds like your voice. There's no distance, no space to argue back.

But when anxiety has a face – when it's a pink spaghetti ball, or whatever absurd creature speaks to you – you can see it as something talking to you, rather than being you.

And once that separation exists, the power dynamic changes.

'It's just a pink spaghetti ball. It's just a pink spaghetti ball. It's just a really loud pink spaghetti ball.'

CHAPTER EIGHT

THE DAY I GOT RICH AND ITCHY

(Or how my pink spaghetti mistress turned champagne into calamine lotion)

There's a scene in *The Shawshank Redemption* that lives rent-free in my head.

Morgan Freeman's character – Ellis Boyd Redding – finally free after forty years, stands beneath that magnificent oak tree in Buxton. He digs up a tin box, opens an envelope and finds the money and letter Andy Dufresne left him. It's beautiful, hopeful – the cinematic embodiment of everything's going to be alright.

I had my own version of that moment.

Picture a Tuesday afternoon on a nondescript high street somewhere in England. I'm standing outside a Greggs – because of course I am; this is Britain, and all significant life moments happen within smelling distance of a sausage roll. My phone is in my hand; my banking app is loading. The sale has gone through. Millions. Millions of pounds.

I watch the digits appear – more zeros than I'd ever

seen attached to my name. Money that would change everything. Money that represented years of grinding, building, selling, sweating, surviving.

This was it. My Morgan Freeman moment.

And do you know what my pink spaghetti mistress did?

She threw a party. A cellular, biological rave so spectacular that within six hours, my hands and feet looked like I'd tried to juggle fire ants while tap-dancing on a wasps' nest.

I developed pompholyx.

For the uninitiated, pompholyx is a stress-induced skin condition where tiny, angry blisters erupt across your palms and soles. It itches like Satan himself is tickling you with a feather made of fibreglass. It weeps. It cracks. It turns the simple act of holding a champagne glass into an exercise in masochism, which was fitting, really, because I wasn't holding any champagne.

THE ANXIETY PARADOX

Here's what's supposed to happen when you sell a company for millions: you call your loved ones, book a table somewhere with cloth napkins, order wine that doesn't have a screw top and toast your success.

Here's what actually happened: I stood on that high street, staring at numbers that should have felt like freedom, while my nervous system reacted as if I'd just been told I had twenty-four hours to defuse a bomb. My heart rate spiked, my breathing shallowed and deep within my endocrine system, my adrenal glands shouted, 'Right lads, he's clearly in mortal danger. Release the cortisol.'

My pink spaghetti mistress looked at the biggest win of my professional life and whispered:

'But what now? What if you lose it? What if they find out you're a fraud? What if this is the peak and everything goes downhill from here? What if, what if, what if ...'

She's romantic like that.

Money doesn't buy happiness

There's a lie that successful people tell themselves: 'Once I hit £X, I'll finally relax.'

I'd invested wholeheartedly in that lie. I'd built an entire internal narrative around the idea that financial security would finally silence the chaos in my skull. But my anxiety didn't get the memo. In fact – and here's the part they skip in self-help books – money can amplify anxiety. Suddenly, you have something to lose. Suddenly, decisions carry real consequences. Suddenly, the stakes aren't theoretical anymore.

When you're skint, anxiety whispers: 'You might fail.' When you're rich, it screams: 'You might fail publicly. From a great height. With witnesses.'

My bank account had changed dramatically. My brain chemistry had not.

THE ITCHY TRUTH

There I was, a newly minted millionaire, sitting in an NHS walk-in clinic at 7 pm, explaining to a very tired nurse that no, I hadn't touched anything unusual, and yes, I understood that stress could manifest physically. I knew I wasn't going to die, but could she please give me something for the itching, because I was losing my mind? She handed me a steroid cream, and off I trotted.

I went home. No champagne. No calls. Just a lukewarm bath – hot water makes pompholyx worse, and my pink spaghetti mistress is nothing if not thorough in her torments. I sat there, wondering why success felt so much like failure.

This is the part where I'm supposed to offer profound insight, wisdom earned through suffering, or a neat bow to tie around this itchy package. But the truth is simpler – and stranger – anxiety doesn't care about net worth. It doesn't respect achievements. It doesn't clock off when you clock off. Anxiety isn't a problem to solve – it's a companion to understand.

My pink spaghetti mistress wasn't punishing me for succeeding. She was doing what she always does, trying to protect me from threats, even when the only threat was my own happiness. She saw joy approaching and, like the bouncer at the world's worst nightclub, decided I wasn't on the list.

CHAPTER NINE

WHAT IS BRAVERY?

'Bravery isn't the absence of fear. It's saying, "Right then, you're here. So am I. Let's figure this out."' – Adam Knights

I've spent twenty-five years trying to answer this question. I've watched men patrol slowly in places where every instinct screamed at them to run. I've seen CEOs stake entire careers on a single decision that could either bankrupt their company or make it. I've watched a single mother in Tesco count out coins for bread while her kids waited, pretending not to notice. And slowly, painfully, I realised something it took me far too long to understand ... bravery isn't what we think it is.

We've been sold a lie about courage. Hollywood gave us square-jawed heroes who never flinch and never doubt themselves when the shooting starts. That's not bravery, that's psychopathy with better lighting.

Cus D'Amato, the man who transformed Mike Tyson from a troubled kid into one of the most feared heavyweights who ever lived, understood this better than anyone. He said something that should be tattooed on the inside of every anxious person's eyelids,

'The hero and the coward both feel the same thing. But the hero uses his fear, projects it onto his opponent, while the coward runs. It's the same thing, fear, but it's what you do with it that matters.'

Read that again. The hero and the coward feel the same dry mouth, the same racing heart, the same voice screaming, 'Get out, get out, get out.' The only difference is what happens next.

I have to admit it: I've been both men. In the Paras, I learned to use fear, to let it sharpen me, to move toward danger because that's what you do, that's what the regiment does and that's what the men beside you are doing. But with my anxiety? I ran.

I ran for years. I avoided situations that might trigger it, made excuses and built my life around not having to face that pink spaghetti mistress when she came calling. I was a coward. There, I've said it. I am a decorated soldier who could advance under fire but couldn't face his own mind. If that isn't darkly hilarious, I don't know what is.

The Stoics understood this two thousand years before Cus D'Amato was born. Marcus Aurelius, the most powerful man in the world, could have spent his days in orgies and excess, but instead spent his nights writing to himself about how to be better.

In his *Meditations* – a book I wish someone had shoved

into my hands at fifteen instead of fifty – he wrote:

'Never let the future disturb you. You will meet it, if you have to, with the same weapons of reason which today arm you against the present.'

And this hit me like a rifle butt to the chest:

'It is not death that a man should fear, but he should fear never beginning to live.'

I'd spent decades fearing my anxiety – fearing the next attack, fearing the fear itself – and in doing so, I'd stopped living whole chunks of my life. I'd handed victory to an enemy that existed only in my own skull.

The Stoics also taught something else: we must face our challenges, not run from them. Seneca, forced to take his own life by a mad emperor, did so with more dignity than most of us manage simply getting out of bed. He put it like this:

'We suffer more often in imagination than in reality.'

Isn't that the whole bloody problem? It wasn't my anxiety killing me – it was the anticipation of my anxiety. The fear of the fear, the running from the running. I'd created an infinite loop of cowardice, and I was the only one who could break it.

So what is bravery, then?

It's not the absence of fear. Anyone who claims they feel no fear is either lying or should probably see a professional. And it's not the suppression of fear either – that just delays the inevitable explosion.

Bravery is feeling the fear and choosing to stay. Choosing

to face it. Choosing to take one more step when every nerve in your body is screaming, retreat, retreat, retreat.

I've seen bravery in a nineteen-year-old private so scared he nearly wet himself yet still he moved to cover his mate under fire. I've seen it in a junior manager who told the CEO her strategy was wrong, fully aware it might end her career. I've seen it in a fifty-five-year-old man finally admitting to his wife that he's been battling panic attacks for twenty-five years.

That last one? That was me. And it was harder than anything I did in uniform.

Even Mike Tyson, the man who terrorised heavyweight boxing for a decade, admitted he was terrified before every fight. But here's what he learned from Cus D'Amato:

'Discipline is doing what you hate to do – but doing it like you love it.'

That's bravery in nine words. It's not about loving the fear – it's about walking into it anyway, with such commitment that an observer might mistake your terror for enthusiasm.

Here's what I've learned about courage after all these years, through every battle, both external and internal:

- Bravery is a practice, not a personality trait. You're not born brave or cowardly
- You become one or the other through repeated choice
- Every time you face something difficult, you strengthen the brave part of you

- Every time you run, you strengthen the coward inside
- Both live within you, waiting to see which one you'll feed today.

And here's the uncomfortable truth I took decades to accept … sometimes you will feel like a coward. Sometimes you will run. Sometimes you will fail. That's not the end of the story, that's just Tuesday. The question is what will you do on Wednesday?

Marcus Aurelius, despite being emperor of Rome, failed constantly. He knew it, he wrote about it, and that's why he kept the *Meditations* private. They were his personal record of shortcomings and of his efforts to do better. He was the most powerful man in the ancient world, yet he wrestled with the same internal battles that we all face every day.

'Waste no more time arguing about what a good man should be. Be one.'

Not 'be one perfectly', nor 'be one without ever failing', but just be one. Start now. Start again. Keep starting.

The bravest thing I've ever done didn't happen in Belfast or the Far East. It wasn't a story that would make a good pub anecdote. It was sitting down with my anxiety – the pink spaghetti mistress who tormented me for years – and saying, 'Right then. You're not going anywhere, and neither am I. So let's figure this out.'

That was the moment I stopped being a coward, not because the fear vanished, because it didn't, but because I finally stopped running.

Cus D'Amato was right … the hero and the coward feel the same thing. The only difference is the direction they face. Turn around.

THE WORDS WE WOUND OURSELVES WITH

Here's something that's been gnawing at me for years, and I reckon it's time someone said it out loud: our language of illness is completely arse over tit.

Pick up any newspaper, any day of the week, and you'll find someone 'battling' cancer. Brave Sarah, 47, is battling breast cancer. Heroic Dave from Croydon is fighting his tumour. Little Timmy is at war with leukaemia.

Battle. Fight. War. Warrior.

I've seen what brutal looks like. I can tell you with absolute certainty that lying in a hospital bed while chemicals drip into your arm isn't a battle. It's not a fight. There's no enemy to outflank, no tactical position to hold and no way to be braver or tougher than your own mutating cells.

- You can't bayonet a tumour.
- You can't outflank chemotherapy.
- You can't call in air support on your own pancreas.

And before you think I'm having a dig, I've had cancer myself! So why do we insist on using combat language? Maybe because it sounds heroic, maybe because it gives us something to do with our fear. But if cancer is a battle, then dying from it becomes a defeat. Suddenly, the poor sod who dies didn't fight hard enough, wasn't brave enough or didn't want it badly enough. What a charming guilt trip to lay on the dying – and their families.

'She lost her battle with cancer.' Lost. She'd fumbled the ball. She'd surrendered.

Now here's where it gets really interesting. Swap diseases and notice the difference. You never read that someone is 'battling anxiety'. Try it: can you imagine a headline like, 'Local Man Wages Heroic War Against His Own Nervous System'? It doesn't exist. Instead, we get: 'Suffers from anxiety'.

Suffers. No battle. No fight. No warrior. Just suffering. Passive, hopeless, eternal suffering. The word sits there like a wet sandbag, pinning you to the ground with zero possibility of movement – a life sentence without parole.

'John suffers from anxiety.' Well, pack it in then, John. Nothing to be done. Off you go to suffer in the corner.

See the madness? Cancer patients get the full military vocabulary; we practically hand out Purple Hearts in oncology. Meanwhile, mental health gets medieval penance. You're not fighting depression – you're afflicted by it. You don't overcome anxiety – you suffer from it. Forever. Amen.

Even the NHS, bless its overstretched cotton socks, is riddled with this linguistic self-harm.

Let me tell you about a visit to a pain clinic. Follow the journey with me:

- You drive to the hospital and park in the Pain Clinic Car Park. First reminder … in case you'd forgotten.
- There's a sign: PAIN. You follow the arrows down the corridor.
- More signs: Pain Management Department. Ah yes, because every nervous system needs a constant visual mantra: Pain. Pain. Pain.
- You sit in the waiting room beneath a poster that says Pain Services.
- You fill out a form about your pain levels.
- Eventually, a nurse calls your name and takes you to see the Pain Consultant.

By the time you sit down, your body has heard the word pain about forty-seven times. Congratulations – you've just been primed, by the healthcare system itself … to feel more pain.

This isn't medicine – it's marketing. And it's marketing against yourself.

Now imagine the same journey, but someone had actually thought about the words:

- You park at the Wellness Centre. You follow signs to Recovery Services.
- You sit beneath a poster about Getting Better.
- You see a Comfort Specialist or a Movement Consultant.

It's the same treatment, the same clinicians, the same medical intervention, but it feels completely different.

Words aren't just noises we make with our mouths – they're instructions, predictions and architects of expectation.

When you tell someone they're going to the Pain Clinic, you're essentially saying: 'Right, off you pop to Pain Town.' That comes with the forecast: painful, with a chance of more pain.

Which brings me to my pink spaghetti mistress, and the linguistic revolution she sparked in my own thick head.

For decades, I would have told you I suffered from anxiety, because it was accurate. I'd wake at 2 am with my heart pounding, lie there with my chest tight, and watch my mind race through catastrophic scenarios. Meetings looked like firing squads. Simple decisions spiralled into paralysing indecision.

It's obviously suffering. What else would you call it?

But here's the thing about suffering: it's a passive verb. You don't 'do suffering'. Suffering happens to you. You're the object, not the subject. The nail, not the hammer.

I got tired of being a nail, so I changed one word:

- I stopped saying I 'suffer from' anxiety
- I started saying I 'benefit from' anxiety.

You can laugh if you want, but here's the darkly funny truth: it works.

- **I benefit** from having my anxiety mistress riding alongside. The hypervigilance that used to torture me now makes me an excellent risk assessor. While other executives are blindly optimistic about projections, I've already imagined seventeen ways the deal could go sideways, and built contingencies for each one.

- **I benefit** from the long conversations we have during those 2 am boardroom meetings, reviewing every threat, every vulnerability, every way the universe might be planning to shaft us. Exhausting? Yes. Thorough? Absolutely. Nothing gets past us.
- **I benefit** from the chest-pounding wake-up calls, because now I know what they are. Just her, tapping me on the shoulder, saying, 'Oi, pay attention – something's happening.' It's not a heart attack or death. It's information. Annoying, yes. Useful, definitely.

'I suffer from anxiety' is a prison sentence.

'I benefit from anxiety' is a job description.

It's the same condition – but a completely different life.

My pink spaghetti mistress hasn't gone anywhere; she still shows up uninvited. She still makes me sweat through shirts before important presentations, and she still catastrophises. However, she's no longer a disease I'm suffering from.

She's a difficult, high-maintenance employee, prone to overtime and terrible boundaries, but now, she works for me. And it's all because I changed the words I use.

So here's my challenge to you, and to the entire healthcare establishment, while we're at it: audit your language.

- Find the battles you're not actually fighting.
- Find the suffering you might be choosing.
- Find the pain clinics that could be recovery centres.
- Find the victims who could be participants.
- Find the hopelessness that could be hard-won wisdom.

The stories we tell ourselves, in the words we select, become our lives.

I used to suffer from anxiety. Now, I benefit from it – from the strangest, most irritating, most valuable relationship of my life. It's the same mistress, just a different dictionary.

CHAPTER TEN

THE LOVE LANGUAGE OF ANXIETY AND MY PINK SPAGHETTI MISTRESS

'Anxiety doesn't disappear when you fight it. It just fights back harder. But when you turn to it and say, "Alright, you're here. Let's do this," it loses its edge.' – Adam Knights

Every relationship has its love languages, and anxiety is no different. Here's what I've learned about speaking anxiety's language:

- **It responds to calm acknowledgement.** 'Hello, you. I see you there.' When you greet anxiety like an old friend rather than a home invader, it loses some of its power. You're not being dismissive, not terrified – you're simply noticing it.
- **It hates being ignored.** Push anxiety down, and it pushes back harder. Pretend it doesn't exist, and it will make itself impossible to ignore. A few minutes of attention now is better than hours of it demanding

your focus later.

- **It speaks in sensations.** Anxiety doesn't use words. It communicates through your body: tight chest, racing heart, shallow breathing. Learn to translate the signals. If your chest feels tight and you feel unsafe, ask yourself, 'What do I need right now?'
- It calms when you stop adding to it. Anxiety is bad enough on its own; anxiety about anxiety makes it unbearable. Drop the second layer and focus on the first.
- **It needs reassurance, not evidence.** Logic rarely works. I've tried it. 'The statistics say I'm fine' has never calmed an anxious brain. Emotional reassurance is what works: 'I've felt this before. I was okay then. I'll be okay now.'

UNDERSTANDING WHAT ANXIETY WANTS

Here's a secret no one tells you: your anxiety isn't trying to hurt you – it's trying to protect you.

I know ... I didn't believe this either. For years, I was convinced anxiety was a sadistic little gremlin, bent on making my life miserable. In reality, it's more like an overprotective grandmother convinced every stranger is a murderer and every aeroplane is a death-trap. Annoying? Absolutely. But it comes from a place of twisted, suffocating, utterly irrational love.

Your nervous system is ancient – antique, really – about

200,000 years old. It evolved when the biggest threats were sabre-toothed tigers, rival tribes ready to bash your head in with rocks and the very real possibility that your dinner might eat you first. Back then, anxiety was useful.

If you heard a rustle in the bushes, your body flooded with adrenaline and cortisol, preparing you to fight or flee at Olympic speed. The anxious cavemen survived. The relaxed ones … didn't.

Congratulations, you're descended from the nervous wrecks.

The problem is that evolution moves at a snail's pace, and your nervous system hasn't got the memo that we're not on the savannah anymore. It's still scanning for predators and preparing you for combat while you're trying to answer emails. It's running ancient software on modern hardware, and the result is that your body treats a LinkedIn notification with the same urgency as a charging rhino.

When anxiety kicks in, your body is essentially screaming: 'DANGER! THREAT DETECTED! PREPARE FOR COMBAT!'

The fact that the 'danger' is an upcoming meeting with HR doesn't matter because your body can't tell the difference. As far as your nervous system is concerned, that meeting might as well be a sabre-toothed tiger wearing a lanyard. It prepares you in the same familiar way: your heart races, your palms sweat, your bowels loosen (thanks for that one, evolution) and you develop a sudden, overwhelming urge to either punch something or sprint towards the nearest exit.

Neither of these responses is particularly helpful in a modern office environment.

It's like having a smoke alarm that goes off every time you make toast. The first few times, you panic. You check for fire, you wave a tea towel at the ceiling, your heart pounds. But eventually, you just stand there, resigned, arm aching, while that infernal beeping drills into your skull and you think, This is my life now.

Annoying, yes, but is it trying to burn your house down? No. It's trying to save you. It's just catastrophically bad at telling the difference between genuine danger and slightly burnt bread.

That's when I realised my anxiety isn't a monster – it's a cavewoman who's been teleported into the twenty-first century and is absolutely losing her mind.

MY PINK SPAGHETTI MISTRESS

She has been living in my nervous system for forty-odd years, and she has no idea what's going on. She was trained for one very specific job: keeping me alive in a hostile wilderness. Now she's been dropped into a world of smartphones, motorways and quarterly performance reviews.

She's confused, stressed and doing her absolute best with a skill set that became obsolete roughly ten thousand years ago.

Every time I open my email, she sees predators. Every notification is a threat. Every meeting is a tribal challenge for dominance. That car that cut me off on the M4? My pink spaghetti mistress wanted to chase it down and establish territorial superiority. The weird look my boss gave me last Tuesday? My pink spaghetti mistress spent the next three nights preparing for exile from the tribe – which, in her mind, means certain death.

She has one mode: EMERGENCY.

She doesn't have settings for 'minor inconvenience', 'probably nothing' or 'this is actually quite a nice day.' She has a big red button that says PANIC, and she hits it with the enthusiasm of a child who's just discovered the hotel lift – again and again and again at the slightest provocation.

- You've got a presentation tomorrow … PANIC
- There's a bill you haven't opened … PANIC
- Someone you don't recognise followed you on Instagram … PANIC, POTENTIAL ENEMY. GATHER INTELLIGENCE

It's exhausting, but I had to learn something that took me years to understand: My spaghetti lover isn't the enemy. She's just an outdated security system designed for a world that no longer exists, running threat assessments on things she doesn't understand. She doesn't know what a mortgage is, but she knows it sounds dangerous. She doesn't understand tax returns, but she's fairly certain they could kill us.

Once I understood this, something shifted. I stopped seeing my anxiety as a malicious force trying to destroy me and started seeing it for what it actually is: an overzealous security guard tackling everyone who approaches the building. She's not trying to ruin things. She's trying to protect the perimeter. She's just comically, tragically, spectacularly bad at assessing actual risk.

My anxiety is like hiring a bouncer from 10,000 BC to work the door at a wine bar. She doesn't know what a wine bar is, and she doesn't understand why people are drinking fermented grapes instead of the mead they brewed in a cave. All she knows is this: strangers are approaching, strangers mean danger and danger means it's time to bare teeth and reach for the club.

'Everyone's a threat,' she growls, squaring up to a middle-aged woman who just wants a Pinot Grigio.

'That's Deborah from marketing,' I try to explain. 'She's not a threat. She's here for the networking event.'

'Networking?' Her eyes narrow ... 'Sounds like a trap.'

'It's just people exchanging business cards.'

'Exchanging what?' She squints. 'They're weapons, aren't they?'

This is what it's like inside my head. Constantly.

But here's what changed: I stopped fighting. I stopped screaming at her to shut up. Instead, I started acknowledging her.

'Thank you,' I began saying to my anxiety. 'I see what

you're trying to do. But I've got this one.'

The first time I said it, I felt like a complete idiot. I was sitting in a toilet cubicle at a conference, heart racing before a panel discussion, essentially talking to my own nervous system as if it were a person. But something interesting happened. The panic didn't disappear –but it softened. It was as if my pink spaghetti mistress had been standing there, club raised, ready to fight, and someone had finally acknowledged her existence.

'Oh. You can see me?'

'Yes, my pink lover. I can see you.'

'And you understand I'm just trying to help?'

'I understand you think you're trying to help.'

'So you're not going to ignore me anymore?'

'No. But I need you to understand something. This panel discussion isn't a tribal council deciding my fate. Those audience members aren't rival warriors sizing me up for battle. The microphone isn't going to electrocute me. And even if I stumble over my words, no one is going to drag me outside and leave me to die in the wilderness.'

'You sure?'

'Reasonably sure, yes.'

'Because I've been monitoring that bloke in the front row, and he looks shifty.'

'He's just tired. It's been a long conference.'

'I've got my eye on him.'

'Of course you do.'

This is the negotiation now. Every day, in every anxious moment, she sounds the alarm. And instead of panicking alongside her or screaming at her to stop, I acknowledge her. I see what she's doing. I understand why she's doing it. And then I gently explain that the email from my accountant is not a declaration of war, and that being left on 'read' doesn't mean the tribe has rejected me.

It doesn't always work. Some days she is absolutely convinced we're about to die, and no amount of gentle reasoning will talk her down. Those are the bad days – the days when the cavewoman wins – and I spend hours preparing for disasters that will never come, fighting enemies that don't exist and fleeing from threats that are entirely imaginary.

But on the good days – and there are more of those now – I can almost feel fondness for this panicked little cave-dweller, desperately trying to keep me safe with the only tools she has. She doesn't know that the world has changed, and she doesn't understand that most of the things she fears can't actually hurt me. She's just doing what our ancestors did for hundreds of thousands of years: scanning the horizon for danger and preparing for the worst.

The worst just happens to be a team meeting now instead of a tiger.

'Thank you for looking out for me,' I tell her when the anxiety rises. 'I know you think this is dangerous. I know your whole being is screaming that we need to run or fight or freeze. But this is just a phone call. This is just a social event. This is just life in the twenty-first century, which I know makes no sense to you, but you're going to have to trust me on this one.'

Sometimes she listens, and sometimes she doesn't. But the conversation helps. The acknowledgement helps. And so does the simple act of saying, I see you. I understand you. I appreciate that you're trying to protect me. Now please put down the club.

My pink lover isn't going anywhere. She's part of the package –hardwired into my DNA, a remnant of a world that no longer exists but left its mark on every cell of my nervous system. I can't evict her or upgrade her to modern software, and I can't make her understand that LinkedIn is not a threat, that unanswered emails won't kill me or that the weird look from my boss was probably just indigestion.

What I can do is work with her. I can acknowledge her concerns, thank her for her vigilance and gently explain that no, we don't need to prepare for battle. We just need to get through Tuesday.

Some days, that's enough. Other days, she and I sit in a toilet cubicle together – her with her club raised, me with my heart pounding –both of us doing our best to survive a world neither of us fully understands.

At least we're in it together.

And we are breathing.

CHAPTER ELEVEN

WHY YOUR BRAIN NEEDS YOU TO BREATHE PROPERLY

'You can't defeat your own nervous system. That's like trying to win a fight against your own left arm.' – Adam Knights

At this point, I'm going to teach you how to breathe … I can already hear you saying, 'Adam, I've been breathing for forty-seven years without your help, you patronising tosser.'

Fair point. But if you've ever had anxiety, you'll know exactly what I mean when I say you can wake up feeling like you're trying to suck your own hair through a ten-foot hosepipe with an entire golf course wedged down your throat. Your chest feels like someone parked a Land Rover on it, your lungs have shrunk to the size of two deflated party balloons and every breath feels about as satisfying as licking a stamp.

If that sounds familiar, congratulations – you've been doing it wrong.

So had I, until I stopped fighting my anxiety and started

learning from people whose lives literally depend on breathing correctly.

Before I dive into the techniques that Navy SEALs, SAS operators and other hard bastards use to stay calm, let me explain why proper breathing works. Unlike most self-help woo-woo, this stuff is backed by science – and understanding that science made all the difference for me.

THE SCIENCE BEHIND BREATHING

When you're anxious, your brain's amygdala – the prehistoric alarm system that evolved to keep your ancestors from being eaten – starts screaming: 'DANGER! DANGER! THERE'S A SABRE-TOOTHED TIGER!' The problem is that your amygdala can't tell the difference between an actual tiger and an email from your boss. It just knows something feels wrong and responds accordingly.

This triggers your sympathetic nervous system, the classic 'fight or flight' response. Your heart rate rockets, blood diverts to your muscles, breathing becomes shallow and rapid and adrenaline floods your system.

This is excellent if you need to outrun a predator – but spectacularly unhelpful if you're just trying to survive a Monday morning meeting.

Here's where it gets interesting: your prefrontal cortex, the rational, thinking part of your brain, needs oxygen to function. When you hyperventilate or breathe shallowly, you're literally reducing blood flow to the part of your brain that could calm your amygdala. In other words, you're making yourself stupider while simultaneously becoming more terrified.

But here's the brilliant bit: breathing is the only autonomic function you can consciously control. You can't force your heart rate down, and you can't reason your adrenal glands into submission – but you can control your breathing. And when you do, you can essentially hack your own nervous system.

Slow, controlled breathing activates your parasympathetic nervous system, the 'rest and digest' system, which tells your body: 'Stand down – there are no tigers here.' It lowers cortisol, slows your heart rate, increases blood flow to your prefrontal cortex and literally changes your brain chemistry.

Research from Stanford shows that deliberate breathing increases heart rate variability (HRV), a marker of how resilient your nervous system is to stress. The more you practise, the better your body becomes at handling future freak-outs.

In other words, breathing properly doesn't just feel better in the moment – it rewires your brain to be less anxious over time. And that's why every special forces unit on the planet makes their operators learn this stuff.

BREATHING TECHNIQUES FROM PEOPLE WHO ACTUALLY NEED THEM

Here's what I've learned: if you want to stay calm under pressure, ask someone who literally gets shot at for a living. These techniques aren't from yoga retreats in Bali (though there's nothing wrong with those). They come from people whose lives depend on them.

And if they work for someone about to breach a building full of hostiles, they'll work just as well for you standing in the queue at Tesco, convinced you're about to die.

1. Box Breathing (Tactical Breathing)

Used by Navy SEALs, Special Forces and law enforcement, this is the granddaddy of military breathing techniques. Why 'box' breathing? Because you visualise a box – four equal sides, four equal parts to the breath.

Former Navy SEAL Mark Divine explains he uses it 'in the morning, before a workout, while standing in line, while stuck in traffic, and whenever else I can.'

If it's good enough for someone whose career involves things they can't even tell you about, it's good enough for you.

How to do it:

- Inhale through your nose for 4 seconds
- Hold your breath for 4 seconds
- Exhale slowly through your mouth for 4 seconds
- Hold your lungs empty for 4 seconds

Repeat for 3–5 minutes (or until you feel human again).

Why it works:

The equal intervals and breath-holds regulate your autonomic nervous system. The holding phases let CO_2 build slightly in your blood, which helps reduce anxiety. (Counter-intuitive, I know –hyperventilation actually lowers CO_2, which fuels that panicked feeling.)

A study in *Frontiers in Psychology* found that regular box breathing significantly reduces cortisol levels and improves sustained attention.

When to use it:

Before stressful situations, during mounting anxiety, when you need to focus or in the middle of the night when that weird twinge in your arm has convinced you you're having a heart attack.

2. The Physiological Sigh (Double Inhale)

Used by Stanford researchers – and honestly, anyone who needs to calm down in thirty seconds.

This technique comes from Dr Andrew Huberman at Stanford, and it's my go-to for acute anxiety.

Here's the beautiful thing: your body already does this naturally. You know that involuntary shuddering sigh you take when crying, drifting off to sleep or narrowly avoiding a car accident? That's a physiological sigh – your nervous system resetting automatically. This technique just teaches you to do it deliberately.

How to do it:

- Take a deep breath in through your nose
- At the top, take a second, shorter breath to fully inflate your lungs
- Exhale slowly and completely through your mouth.

Why it works:

Your lungs contain roughly 500 million tiny air sacs called alveoli. Stress and shallow breathing cause many of these to collapse, reducing oxygen exchange and increasing CO_2 levels in your blood. The double inhale reinflates these collapsed alveoli – the second 'top-up' breath is the key.

Meanwhile, the extended exhale activates your vagus nerve, the main highway from your brain to your gut, which is essentially the master switch for your parasympathetic nervous system.

Research backs this up: a randomised controlled trial published in *Cell Reports Medicine* found that cyclic sighing outperformed mindfulness meditation for improving mood.

When to use it:
Use this technique when you need to calm down immediately – for example, in a meeting where you can't excuse yourself, or when your pink spaghetti mistress is whispering catastrophic scenarios in your ear and you need her to shut up for five minutes.

3. The 4-7-8 Technique (The 'Natural Tranquilliser')
This method is used by Dr Andrew Weil, insomniacs everywhere, and anyone who's ever stared at the ceiling at 3 a.m.

Dr Weil calls it a 'natural tranquilliser for the nervous system' –which sounds like marketing bollocks until you try it. The extended breath hold and even longer exhale hit your parasympathetic nervous system hard. I've used this lying in bed at 4 am, convinced the tightness in my chest means I'm dying, and within three cycles, I'm either asleep or at least no longer catastrophising.

How to do it:

- Exhale completely through your mouth (make a 'whoosh' sound if you're alone)
- Inhale quietly through your nose for 4 seconds
- Hold your breath for 7 seconds
- Exhale through your mouth for 8 seconds
- Repeat 4 times (or until you fall asleep or feel calmer).

Why it works:

The 7-second hold lets oxygen saturate your bloodstream while giving CO_2 time to reach optimal levels. The 8-second exhale –longer than the inhale – is the key to triggering the parasympathetic response. Research shows this pattern increases theta and delta brain waves, the same ones present during deep relaxation and sleep, while reducing sympathetic nervous system activity.

When to use it:

Before sleep, during prolonged anxiety or when you've been catastrophising for hours and need a proper reset. Warning: you might feel a little lightheaded at first – start with just four cycles until you're comfortable.

4. Combat Tactical Breathing (The Grossman Method)

Used by the military, law enforcement and first responders, this method is named after Lt Col Dave Grossman, author of *On Combat*, the definitive guide to the psychology and physiology of deadly conflict. Soldiers are trained to deliberately lower their heart rate from stress-induced highs back to baseline within minutes. If they can do it before breaching a building full of hostiles, you can do it before a job interview.

How to do it:

- Inhale through your nose for 4 seconds, visualising the numbers 1, 2, 3, 4
- Hold for 4 seconds, visualising the numbers again
- Exhale through your mouth for 4 seconds, visualising the numbers
- Repeat 3–5 times, or until you feel calm.

Why it works:

The number visualisation gives your conscious mind something to focus on besides the threat – real or imagined – while the rhythmic breathing does the physiological work. Research in *Applied Psychophysiology and Biofeedback* shows tactical breathing improves first-shot accuracy in marksmanship, proving it genuinely enhances performance under stress, not just how you feel.

When to use it:
During acute stress or before high-stakes moments when your fight-or-flight response is triggered. It's also excellent for managing rage – I've used it in traffic more times than I can count.

5. The 2:1 Ratio (Extended Exhale)
Used by Navy SEALs, military performance coaches and the German armed forces.

Sometimes you need something simple – a technique you can do without counting complicated sequences. The 2:1 ratio is exactly as it sounds leukaemia: your exhale is twice as long as your inhale. That's it. It's simple, flexible and adaptable to any situation.

How to do it:

- Inhale through your nose for 3–4 seconds
- Exhale through your mouth for 6–8 seconds.

Why it works:
The extended exhale is the secret ingredient in almost every calming breath technique. Exhaling naturally lowers your heart rate – a phenomenon called respiratory sinus arrhythmia (RSA). By extending your exhale, you literally spend more time in a calmer, lower-heart-rate state.

Research from the German armed forces found that extended exhalation breathing outperformed tactical breathing when active coping was required.

When to use it:
Anytime, anywhere. Perfect for moments when you need something simple you don't have to think about – even during conversations when you can't obviously be doing breathing exercises.

6. Adam's Favourite: The Double-Dip
Used by me … a lot. I've tried every technique: boxed my way into temporary blueness, 4-7-8'd through countless insomniac nights. They all work – but the one I keep coming back to is the Double-Dip. I've never seen it written down exactly like this, so I named it poorly and honestly. It involves inhaling twice.

How to do it:

- Take a deep breath in through your nose
- At the top, quickly snatch another breath on top of it
- Long, slow exhale – if you can
- That's it. One breath, a quick top-up, then a long exhale. No counting, no visualisation – just breathe, top-up and let it out.

Why it works:
After researching this chapter, I realised my instinctive technique is essentially a simplified physiological sigh,

giving me some validation from Stanford neuroscience. The double inhale maximises alveoli reinflation and oxygen uptake, while the extended exhale stimulates the vagus nerve. It's physiologically sound, even if I stumbled on it by accident.

Part of why it works for me is that the extra 'snatch' breath requires active engagement. Anxiety makes breathing shallow and passive – I often feel like I'm being breathed rather than breathing. That extra inhale restores control. It's a tiny act of defiance against panic.

When to use it:

I use it whenever the pink spaghetti mistress gets too loud, when I wake up feeling suffocated or when my chest tightens and thoughts spiral. Meetings, planes, presentations, 3 am – it's become my default reset button.

WHEN TO BREATHE: BEFORE, DURING AND AFTER

Before the storm:

If you know anxiety is coming – during a difficult conversation, public speaking engagement or medical appointment – practise your chosen technique for 3–5 minutes beforehand. Think of it like stretching before exercise: you're prepping your nervous system.

I now do this automatically before anything stressful. Box breathing in the car before a big meeting, 4-7-8 in bed before an important presentation and the Double-Dip in the bathroom before difficult conversations. It's as natural as checking my wallet.

During the chaos:

When anxiety hits mid-situation, you need something quick and discreet.

The physiological sigh – or my Double-Dip version – is perfect because a single breath cycle can shift your state. No one notices, and you can do it while someone is talking to you, reading a distressing email or sitting in a waiting room convinced you're about to die.

The key is catching it early. Intervene as soon as you notice that familiar tightening in your chest, the quickening of your breath and that rising sense of doom. Don't wait until full panic sets in – the earlier you start breathing properly, the easier it is to prevent the avalanche.

AFTER THE FLOOD:

After an anxiety attack – or even just a stressful event – your nervous system doesn't instantly reset. Cortisol is still circulating, and your amygdala is still on high alert. This is when longer breathing practices help. Five to ten minutes of box breathing or the 4-7-8 technique can deactivate your stress response and help your body return to baseline.

I've learned to schedule recovery time after stressful events. If I've had a difficult meeting or a panic-inducing experience, I carve out ten minutes alone just to breathe. It's not indulgent, it's maintenance. Like changing the oil in your car after a long journey.

THE UNCOMFORTABLE TRUTH

Here's the thing no one tells you: breathing techniques feel stupid at first. You'll sit there counting to four, feeling like an absolute tool, wondering how this is supposed to help when your mind is screaming that you're about to die. But eventually, something shifts. Maybe not the first time – or the tenth – but eventually. You'll notice your heart rate dropping, feel that almost physical sense of your nervous system standing down, think more clearly and realise that this strange, simple, slightly embarrassing practice actually works.

Navy SEALs bet their lives on this stuff. Stanford neuroscientists have proven it works. Special Forces units around the world make it mandatory. These are not people prone to wasting time on nonsense.

So the next time you wake up feeling like you're trying to suck your own hair through a hosepipe – or the next time your pink spaghetti mistress starts whispering catastrophes in your ear – remember you have a tool. It's free. It's always available. And it's as fundamental as it gets.

Just breathe … properly, this time.

QUICK REFERENCE: BREATHING TECHNIQUES

- Box Breathing (4-4-4-4): In 4 → Hold 4 → Out 4 → Hold 4

Best for: General anxiety, focus, pre-stress preparation

- Physiological Sigh: Double inhale → Long exhale

Best for: Quick reset, acute stress, discreet use

- 4-7-8 Technique: In 4 → Hold 7 → Out 8

Best for: Sleep, prolonged anxiety, deep relaxation

- Combat Tactical Breathing: In 4 → Hold 4 → Out 4 (with visualisation)

Best for: High-stress situations, performance anxiety

- 2:1 Ratio: In 3–4 → Out 6–8

Best for: Anytime, anywhere, simple and flexible

- The Double-Dip (Adam's Favourite): Deep breath → Quick top-up → Long exhale

Best for: Honestly, everything

Tip: Practise when calm so it becomes automatic under stress. The more you use these techniques, the more effective they get.

PART THREE

THE RELATIONSHIP

(or learning to live with your persistent, unwanted, occasionally useful houseguest)

CHAPTER THIRTEEN

THE DEVIL MAKES WORK (OR WHY TRAINSPOTTERS HAVE IT FIGURED OUT)

'I stopped treating my anxiety like an enemy and started treating it like an uninvited houseguest who wasn't leaving anytime soon.'–Adam Knights

When I sold my last company I thought I'd cracked it. Early retirement, a fat bank account, and absolutely nothing I had to do ever again. I was going to become one of those insufferable people who "'work on their latest project"' and "'finally have time to read."'

I planned to buy ridiculous things, simply because I could – a watch more expensive than my first car, kitchen gadgets designed by people who'd clearly never cooked, and one of those massive outdoor pizza ovens that gets used exactly twice.

For about three glorious weeks, it was perfect. Then it became something else entirely.

There's an old saying: "'The devil makes work for idle hands."'

What nobody mentions is that in my case, the devil wears pink spaghetti – and she'd been waiting patiently for this moment. Through all those busy years, sprinting from meeting to meeting, deal to deal, crisis to crisis, she'd never had a chance to speak. But now? She was ready.

The moment I sat down with nothing to do:

'Hello, darling. Miss me? I've prepared a slideshow.'

Anxiety, I've discovered, is like a cat – not in the cute way, but in the predatory way. She watches, waits and thrives when your mind is idle. A retirement without purpose hands her the keys to your skull and says, 'Go on then, redecorate.'

Within weeks, I found myself sitting on the sofa at 2 pm on a Tuesday, wearing the same clothes I slept in, watching my fourth consecutive episode of something I didn't even like, while a small voice catalogued every poor decision I'd made since 1987. The pizza oven sat outside, unused, silently judging me, and the expensive watch counted down the seconds until the next wave of existential dread. She was having the time of her life.

'Remember when you thought you'd be happy doing nothing?' she whispered. 'Funny, that. Shall we discuss your childhood? Your mates getting badly injured in Belfast? That thing you said at the Christmas party in 2003? I've got time – and clearly, so do you.'

WHAT DID I DO NEXT?

I started writing books and launched a new company.

Not because I thought I had any talent – the jury's still out – but because I needed something to occupy the mental real estate she'd been squatting in. I needed focus, structure, problems to solve and fires to put out. I needed the sense that a day had a purpose beyond 'exist' and 'try not to spiral.'

Bit by bit, she retreated – not entirely, because she never leaves completely – but she went from a constant, uninvited house guest to something more manageable: an occasional visitor, someone who pops in after a quiet few days, taps me on the shoulder and says, 'Just checking you haven't forgotten I exist. Anyway, remember that time you …'

'Yes, yes,' I reply. 'But I'm in the middle of something. Can this wait?'

She hates being deprioritised, but she can't argue with it. When you're genuinely engaged, fully focused and present, she struggles to get a foothold. Anxiety needs empty space to operate, silence to fill, a vacuum to rush into. Take away the vacuum, and she's got nowhere to go.

It's insane – and, ironically, it's also terrible leadership. Here's what I've learned, the hard way, over years of both having anxiety and leading people who do: anxiety isn't weakness. It's awareness. It's pattern recognition. It's your brain trying – sometimes clumsily – to keep you safe from things that have hurt you before.

When you stop fighting it and start listening, anxiety becomes a slightly neurotic, occasionally overwhelming co-pilot. One who needs firm management and regular breaks, yes, but a co-pilot, nonetheless.

The people I know with anxiety are often the most perceptive in the room. They notice things others miss, anticipate problems before they materialise and are seventeen steps ahead because their brains are wired for threat detection. With the right framing, it's a superpower.

The problem isn't the anxiety itself – it's that most workplaces give you nothing to do with it except suppress it, hide it and pretend you're one of the 'normal' ones who doesn't have a small pink demon screaming predictions of doom every time the boss calls an unscheduled meeting.

What I've discovered is that my anxiety responds to being needed. She calms down when there's real, meaningful work to do – the kind of work that engages enough of my brain that she can't get a word in.

When I'm in the middle of something that matters – genuinely locked in, solving problems, creating things, pushing towards a goal – she takes a back seat. She might still be there, watching, occasionally even helpful. 'Have you considered that risk?' she'll murmur, and for once it's useful instead of paralysing.

But the moment I stop, hit a lull or drift into a quiet patch, she's back. It's like she has a sensor for purpose: when you have it, she respects it; when you don't, she fills the void.

Here's the thing about fulfilment and anxiety that nobody told me and I had to figure it out by making expensive mistakes and enduring many unwanted 3 am slide presentations: they're inversely proportional.

The more fulfilled you are, the less space anxiety has to operate. The less fulfilled you are, the more she expands to fill the gap. Give her your whole life, and she'll fill it. Give her a small corner – because the rest is occupied with things that matter to you – and she'll sulk there, occasionally throwing things, but mostly staying contained.

This doesn't mean you need to 'stay busy'. Busy is different. Busy is answering emails you don't care about, attending meetings that could have been emails, ticking boxes on someone else's list. Busy keeps your hands occupied but leaves your mind wide open for her to move in. I've been busy and miserable, busy and anxious, busy and empty.

Fulfilment is different. It's doing things that matter to you, that engage you, that make time irrelevant because you're fully immersed. Find those things, build your life around them and watch her influence shrink.

CHAPTER FOURTEEN

LIGHTENING THE LOAD

'Stop trying to conquer your feelings.
Start trying to understand them.' – Adam Knights

Living with anxiety is a bit like carrying a rucksack full of bricks. You can't put it down – we've established that – but over time, you can figure out ways to make the load a little lighter or at least make your legs stronger. Or you can learn to distract yourself from the weight long enough to enjoy the walk.

What follows is not a prescription. I'm not a doctor, a therapist or anyone with letters after their name that would qualify me to tell you what to do. I'm just a bloke who's been hauling this rucksack for a few decades and has worked out through extensive trial and error, what makes my days slightly less mental.

WHAT I STOPPED DOING

The first thing I stopped doing was drinking. The simple truth is that it wasn't serving me. That's it. There was no dramatic rock-bottom moment. I just noticed that, over time, alcohol and anxiety were having a little party together – and I wasn't invited.

Here's what nobody really tells you about alcohol and anxiety: they're mates. They're the sort of mates who egg each other on, make everything worse and still manage to convince you they're helping.

WHAT I DO INSTEAD

Every morning, without fail, I have a coffee. Rituals, as it turns out, are incredibly important when you're managing anxiety. They're small anchors – signals to your brain that say: this is normal, this is safe, we've done this before and we survived.

After the coffee comes the bit that makes people look at me like I've lost my mind: the cold pod. I've got a cold-water pod in my garden, and every morning I climb into it and sit there for about four minutes. The water is properly cold – cold enough that the first thirty seconds involve noises that would concern the neighbours if they could hear them.

What I do know is this: when I get out of that pod – shaking, gasping and feeling more alive than any reasonable person should feel at seven in the morning – my anxiety is quieter. Not gone. Never gone. But quieter.

Then there's the walking. I walk every day, without exception – rain, shine, sleet or that weird drizzly fog that Britain specialises in.

And here's what I've learned: it doesn't matter how far you go. It could be a hundred yards or a hundred miles; they both work. The act of moving – of putting one foot in front of the other, of being out in the world instead of trapped in your own head – does something.

FEAR IS A WASTED EMOTION

After two decades of living with anxiety, I've discovered that once you build a relationship with it – once you've sat down and had those mad conversations I talked about earlier – fear starts to lose its power. You begin to see it for what it is: anxiety's favourite toy.

Once you've seen the trick, it's harder to be fooled by it.

'He who fears death will never do anything worthy of a man who is alive.' – Seneca

The Stoics were obsessed with death, which sounds morbid until you realise what they were getting at. If you spend your life fearing the worst thing that could happen, you don't actually live – you just exist in a permanent state of waiting for disaster.

Fear is a thief. It doesn't just steal your peace of mind in the moment; it steals entire chunks of your life. Every experience you avoided, every opportunity you didn't take, every conversation you didn't have, every flight you didn't board – it all gets tallied up.

The bill is your unlived life.

'It is not because things are difficult that we do not dare; it is

because we do not dare that things are difficult.'– Seneca

This one took me years to understand. I used to think brave people simply weren't afraid, that courage was the absence of fear. That turns out to be complete bollocks. Courage isn't the absence of fear; it's the decision that something else matters more.

The Parachute Regiment taught me that. You think anyone wants to jump out of a perfectly good aircraft? Of course not. But the mission matters more than the fear. The bloke beside you matters more than the fear. Getting the job done matters more than the fear.

So you jump.

And here's what nobody tells you: the fear before the jump is always worse than the jump itself. Every single time.

DARK NIGHTS OF THE SOUL

Not every day is a victory, so let's be honest about that. Some nights, the 2 am tap isn't a gentle nudge but a full-blown assault. Some days, the physical symptoms are so overwhelming that the idea of falling in love with them feels like a sick joke. Some weeks, it feels like you're right back at square one, wondering if any of it has made a difference at all.

I've had those nights, those days, those weeks … and I still do, occasionally. This isn't a fairy tale where the hero slays the dragon and lives happily ever after. This is real life, where the dragon moves in permanently and sometimes sets fire to the curtains at 3 am because it's bored.

Here's something that still baffles me, twenty-five years after leaving the Army.

I spent nine amazing years in the Army. Nine years of cold nights in places designed to kill you. I've lain in ditches in East Tyrone with rain seeping through my smock, knowing that any shadow could be a sniper, any parked car could be a bomb and any teenager walking past could be carrying a message – or a weapon. I've done jungle training in the Far East, where the humidity tried to drown you and everything that moved wanted to eat you. I've been in Africa, in the strangest situations.

And through all of it – every freezing observation post, every nerve-shredding patrol, every moment where my life genuinely hung in the balance – I coped. I functioned. I did my job. I slept when I could and stayed alert when I needed to be alert. My nervous system performed exactly as required.

Yet somehow, in my beautiful farmhouse in the English countryside, with central heating, a memory-foam mattress and absolutely zero probability of being shot at, I've had some of the worst nights of my entire life.

Explain that one. I've genuinely tried.

I've lain there at 2 am, heart racing, chest tight, convinced something terrible was about to happen, and thought to myself: Mate. You've slept in a shell scrape in the Ardboe while the IRA were conducting an active service operation somewhere in the darkness. You've done fortyeight-hour observation posts in freezing rain. You once woke up in central Africa with a spider the size of a dinner plate on your sleeping bag – and calmly flicked it off and went back to sleep.

And yet here you are, in a heated bedroom, under a goose down duvet, with your wife breathing peacefully beside you, and you're bloody terrified.

Of what?

Exactly. Of what?

I remember one night in Northern Ireland. It was the winter of 1992, and we were on an OP – an observation post – lying in wait in a concealed position, watching a location where intelligence suggested weapons might be moved.

They'd picked a drainage ditch alongside a field, about two hundred metres from a farmhouse. It was pissing down, and the temperature hovered just above freezing – too warm to die of hypothermia, but too cold to feel your extremities. The ditch slowly filled with water despite our best efforts, and by hour three I was essentially lying in a shallow bath of freezing mud.

We couldn't move. We couldn't light a fire, obviously, and we couldn't even shift position without risking compromise. We just lay there, motionless, watching and waiting, while the rain hammered down and the cold crept deeper into our bones.

And here's the thing: I was fine.

Uncomfortable as hell, yes. Questioning my life choices, certainly. But mentally, I was completely stable. My heart rate was normal. My breathing was easy. I wasn't anxious at all.

I was just doing the job.

The operation lasted eight hours. We got nothing. No movement at the farmhouse, no weapons transfer – just a lot of wet misery and a debrief where we all pretended we hadn't spent the night lying in a bog.

I went back to base, had a hot shower, ate something questionable from the cookhouse and slept like the dead. There was no anxiety. No panic. Nothing.

Fast forward twenty-five years.

I'm in my farmhouse. I've had a lovely dinner, watched some television and gone to bed in a room that costs more to heat each month than my entire Army salary once did. The sheets are Egyptian cotton. There's a glass of water on the bedside table. My wife is reading beside me. A dog is snoring at the foot of the bed.

And suddenly, without warning, without reason, my body decides I'm in mortal danger.

My heart rate goes through the roof. My chest tightens like a drum. My breathing turns rapid and shallow. My hands tingle. My vision narrows. The full fight-or-flight response is deployed against the terrifying threat of what, exactly? An Aga and some nice furniture?

I've thought about this paradox a lot, and the best explanation I can come up with is this: in Belfast, in Africa, in all those dangerous places, there was an actual threat. My nervous system had something real to respond to. The danger was external, identifiable and – most importantly – I could do something about it. I had training. I had equipment. I had mates watching my back. I was in control or at least had the illusion of it.

Anxiety doesn't work that way.

There's no external enemy to shoot at, no mission to complete, no extraction point to reach. It's all internal. All invisible. And you can't fight your own nervous system with a GPMG (general purpose machine gun). Believe me, I've tried.

The dark nights are the hardest. There's something about 2 am that anxiety absolutely loves. It's like a vampire – strongest in the darkness when you're alone with your thoughts and there's nothing left to distract you.

I call it the 2 am tap. It's the moment you're wrenched from sleep by your body's absolute conviction that something is terribly wrong. Sometimes it's gentle, just a low hum of unease that slowly builds. Other times it's like being hit with a cattle prod. One moment you're peacefully unconscious; the next you're bolt upright, your heart trying to escape through your ribcage.

On the bad nights, my pink spaghetti mistress doesn't just tap. She kicks the door in with a battering ram, flicks on all the lights and starts blasting a brass-band medley of my greatest failures at full volume.

'Remember that business decision you made in 2003? Let's examine that in excruciating detail.'

'What about that thing you said to your father in 1997? Shall we revisit that?'

'And have you considered all the ways your body could be failing right now without your knowledge? Let me count them.'

She's thorough, I'll give her that. If anxiety were a profession, she'd be employee of the month every single month. No detail is too small to catastrophise, no worry too absurd to investigate, and by 4 am we've usually covered my entire life history, several hypothetical future disasters that haven't happened yet, and at least three rare diseases I'm apparently developing based on a slight twinge in my left knee.

I had one particularly memorable dark night about three years ago. The business was going through a slightly rough patch, but my anxiety had decided this was The End of Everything.

I awoke at 2:17 am. I know the exact time because I stared at the clock for what felt like hours while my nervous system ran through its entire repertoire of horrors. Heart palpitations. Chest tightness. Numb hands. The works.

Sometime around 3 am, in the depths of my misery, I had a thought that was either profound or completely unhinged. Possibly both.

Right now, at this exact moment, I thought, there's probably some young Para in a trench somewhere, rain hammering down, cold seeping into his bones, genuinely not knowing if he'll survive the night, and he's probably sleeping better than me.

I laughed, in the middle of a panic attack. At 3 am, no less. I laughed because it was true, and because it was absurd. And sometimes absurdity is the only honest response to the cosmic joke of anxiety.

Here I was: a fifty-something man who had survived actual combat, actual danger, actual life-threatening situations, now being terrorised by his own brain chemistry in a heated bedroom. The irony was so thick you could spread it on toast.

There's a written list I keep of all the times I was certain something terrible was happening, and it turned out to be anxiety. It's a long list now, and reading it helps on the dark nights:

- The time I was convinced I had a brain tumour because of persistent headaches. Wasn't that. It was tension from grinding my teeth.
- The time I thought I was having a heart attack in Marks & Spencer. Wasn't that either. Just anxiety doing its cardiac impression.
- The time my legs went numb, and I was certain I had MS. Nope. Anxiety again – the theatrical bastard.

- The time at the airport when I was convinced I had a pulmonary embolism. False alarm. Just anxiety having a field day with the stress of travel.
- The time I cancelled a holiday because I was absolutely certain I wouldn't survive the flight. I did survive. Still annoyed about missing Tuscany.

The list goes on, and on, and on. It's a comprehensive catalogue of anxiety's greatest hits – each one a moment when I was utterly convinced the end was nigh, and each one further proof that my predictions of doom have an almost perfect failure rate.

That's the thing about catastrophising: it's remarkably consistent in being wrong. If anxiety were a weather forecaster, it would be fired. If it were a financial adviser, it would be in prison. And yet, night after night, we keep believing it – like this time it's finally going to be right.

The difference now is that, after years of practice and after learning to fall in love with my anxiety rather than fight it, I don't add despair to the suffering.

This matters, so I'll say it again: I don't add despair to the suffering.

Before, when the dark nights came, I would lie there thinking, I'll never get better. What's the point of all this work I've done? I'm fundamentally broken and always will be.

This is my life now – forever – an endless series of 2 am terror attacks until I finally die of exhaustion or embarrassment.

That kind of thinking takes a bad night and turns it apocalyptic. It's suffering about suffering, fear about fear – the feedback loop that turns a wave into a tsunami.

Now, when the dark nights come, I think something much simpler: This is a bad one. It will pass.

Because it always does. I've never had a panic attack that lasted forever, and I've never had anxiety that didn't eventually fade. Even the worst episodes have an end. The wave crests, then recedes. That's what waves do.

On those nights, I remind myself of my track record. I've survived every single panic attack I've ever had. Think about that – every single one. My survival rate is one hundred per cent. I've made it through the mild ones and the horrific ones, the ones that made me question my sanity. I'm still here, still breathing, still functioning.

They're not bad odds when you think about it.

MY WORST DARK NIGHT

Let me tell you about the worst dark night I can remember.

It was about six years ago, and everything was going wrong at once – business pressures, family stuff, health worries, the full catastrophe. I'd been just about managing, using all the techniques I'd learned, keeping my head above water. But that night, everything collapsed.

I didn't just wake up at 2 am, I never really slept. The anxiety had been building all day like a thunderstorm on the horizon, and by bedtime it was ready to unleash.

The physical symptoms were overwhelming. My heart was doing things that should require medical attention. My chest felt like someone was standing on it. My hands were numb, my vision was strange and I was completely convinced that this was it – that this time it wasn't anxiety, but the real thing.

Goodbye, cruel world.

I got up because I couldn't lie still. I went downstairs and paced around the kitchen like a caged animal, trying to decide whether to call an ambulance or just wait to die. The dog followed me, confused by the midnight walkabout but loyal enough to participate. She kept looking at me with that expression dogs have – part concern, part 'Is this when we eat?'

At some point, I found myself standing by the window, staring out into the darkness, talking out loud to my anxiety.

'Alright,' I said. 'You've got me. You win. I can't fight this anymore. Do your worst.'

It was surrender – but not the healthy, mindful acceptance I'd been practising. This was full white-flag surrender. I was too exhausted to fight, too tired to care and too depleted to do anything except give in completely.

And here's the strange thing.

It started to ease.

Not immediately – gradually. The peak passed. The wave crested. The symptoms began, slowly, to subside.

By 4 am, I was back in bed. I wasn't sleeping, just lying

there in the aftermath, like a beach after a storm. There was debris everywhere, but the worst was over.

By 6 am, I slept. Not well, but I slept.

By morning, I was alive. Still here. Still breathing, still able to get up, have breakfast and face another day.

The dark night had done its worst – and I'd survived. Again. I added it to the list.

There's something my old dad used to say that's stuck with me: 'It's always darkest before the dawn.'

The night is long, but it always ends. And dawn always comes.

Not because you've done anything to deserve it. Not because you've figured out the secret. Not because you've finally conquered your demons. It comes because that's what dawn does. It's relentless, inevitable – a cosmic promise that no amount of darkness can break.

I think about those young Paras sometimes – the ones out there right now in some godforsaken corner of the world, lying in ditches, watching and waiting, enduring conditions that would break most people. They don't know it yet, but most of them will cope just fine in those moments … and then struggle inexplicably years later in heated bedrooms, with no enemy in sight.

That's the cruel joke of anxiety.

It waits. It picks its moment. It attacks when you're safe, not when you're in danger. It saves its best work for when you've finally got everything you thought you wanted – the comfortable life, the successful career, the beautiful home.

Then it whispers, 'Congratulations. Now let's discuss everything that could go wrong.'

But here's what I've learned, after all these years and these dark nights: you can survive it. You have survived it – every single time. Your record is perfect.

It's undefeated.

The dark nights still come for me, and probably always will. My pink spaghetti mistress isn't going anywhere. She's too comfortable in the spare room and far too attached to her collection of my fears and failures.

But they don't stay as long anymore. And they don't dig as deep.

Because I've learned not to fight them. Not to add despair to the suffering. Not to catastrophise about catastrophising.

I just wait for dawn.

And dawn – bless it – has never once let me down.

CHAPTER FIFTEEN

THE WALK THAT CHANGED EVERYTHING

(How I stopped running from myself and started walking instead)

About six months into my new approach to anxiety, I was walking through the countryside near my home when it arrived – uninvited, familiar and relentless. My heart raced, my vision narrowed and that old sense of impending doom settled in.

The old me would have turned around, gone home and hidden. The new me said, 'Alright. Let's walk.'

So I walked with it. I didn't try to breathe it away, think it away or fight it. I simply let it be there alongside me. And something strange happened: it didn't escalate. Normally, anxiety would feed on my fear, building momentum until it felt unstoppable. This time, without fear to fuel it, it just … sat there. Uncomfortable, yes, but static.

After about twenty minutes, it began to fade. Not because I had done anything, but because anxiety can't sustain itself forever without fuel. By refusing to resist it, I had stopped feeding it.

I remember pausing on a hillside, looking out over the valley, and laughing. Not because it was funny, but because I had finally understood something profound: anxiety is only as powerful as the resistance you give it.

When I stop resisting, it loses most of its power. The anxiety itself – just sensations – is still uncomfortable, but the horror, dread and the conviction that I'm dying come from the fight, not from the feelings themselves. The suffering, I realised, is optional.

WHY WALKING WORKS (AND IT'S NOT JUST ABOUT 'GETTING EXERCISE')

I could have just said, 'Walking makes me feel better' and left it at that. That's the kind of advice people throw at you when they have nothing useful to offer: 'Just go for a walk, mate.'

But here's the thing: walking actually works for anxiety, and there's solid science behind it. Understanding that science made me take it seriously, so bear with me while I get a little nerdy …

1. Your brain's free drug cabinet

When you walk at a decent pace, your brain does something remarkable: it releases endorphins. You've probably heard of them – they're your body's natural painkillers and mood elevators. Chemically, they're similar to morphine – but free, and without the risk of ending up in a ditch in Moss Side.

Harvard research shows that even a twenty-minute walk can clear your mind and reduce stress. Endorphins flood your system, binding to the same receptors that opiates target, creating what some researchers call a 'natural high'. This isn't woo-woo wellness speak – it's measurable neurochemistry.

Walking doesn't stop there. It also increases serotonin – the neurotransmitter antidepressants aim for – and boosts brain-derived neurotrophic factor (BDNF), which acts like a fertiliser for neurons. BDNF promotes new brain cell growth, especially in the hippocampus – the part of the brain responsible for emotional regulation and memory.

In other words: walking literally repairs and strengthens your brain. And all it costs is a pair of decent shoes and twenty minutes of your time.

2. The stress hormone gets its arse kicked

Here's something fascinating: anxiety triggers your body to pump out cortisol, the primary stress hormone. It's useful in real emergencies – giving you a burst of energy to run from a burning building or defend yourself. But chronically elevated cortisol, as happens with anxiety, wreaks havoc.
High cortisol suppresses the immune system, disrupts sleep, causes weight gain around the middle, impairs memory – and ironically, fuels more anxiety. It's a vicious cycle: anxiety creates cortisol, and cortisol creates anxiety. Walking breaks that cycle.

Studies show that just twenty minutes of brisk walking significantly lowers cortisol levels. Your body gets the message: 'We are not under threat. We can stand down.' When cortisol drops, so does that constant background hum of dread that anxious people know all too well.

3. The ping-pong effect (EMDR without the therapist's bill)

Here's something that genuinely surprised me: have you heard of EMDR therapy? It stands for Eye Movement Desensitisation and Reprocessing and is a gold-standard treatment for trauma and PTSD, used by the NHS and military psychologists worldwide.

The core mechanism is bilateral stimulation – rhythmic, alternating stimulation of both sides of the brain.

Guess what walking is? Bilateral stimulation. Left foot, right foot. Left arm swings, right arm swings. The alternating rhythm activates both hemispheres of your brain, improving communication between them and helping process emotional experiences.

Research shows that this type of bilateral movement reduces the emotional charge of traumatic or distressing memories. The memory doesn't disappear – you'll still remember that anxiety hit you on a Tuesday afternoon – but it loses its power. It becomes information rather than experience.

This explains why walking while anxious feels different

from sitting with anxiety. Sitting with anxiety is like being trapped in a small room with it. Walking with anxiety feels like having a difficult conversation with a companion while moving through the world. Same anxiety. Different relationship. And that movement changes everything.

4. Adam's secret weapon: The head torch

Here's a tip that might sound odd, but I'm deadly serious: buy a proper head torch. Not a cheap pound-shop thing that dies after twenty minutes. Get a decent LED one with strong battery life and a reliable beam – you can grab a good model for around thirty quid, and it will change your life.

Here's why. In Britain, from October to March, it's dark by 4 pm – and even earlier in December. For most people working normal hours that means your outdoor time is either squeezed into weekends or spent in darkness. Many of us just stop going outside, hibernate indoors, doomscroll and then wonder why we feel miserable.

A head torch makes the darkness irrelevant. I've walked across fields at 7 pm on a January evening, breath freezing in the air, the torch beam illuminating the path ahead and felt more alive than I do in summer. There's something almost magical about night walking: the world feels different, quieter and more intimate.

Night walks are also incredibly calming for anxiety, on your own or in a small group. The darkness reduces visual stimulation, giving your hypervigilant brain less to scan and assess. The cold air wakes you up and grounds you in your body, and the silence – broken only by the occasional owl or suspicious rustle (probably just a badger) – is meditative.

Even in winter, evening walks are now non-negotiable for me. When anxiety hits, I don't wait for daylight. I strap on my head torch and walk twenty minutes across the fields behind my house – thirty if the anxiety is high. I return cold, mud-splattered, and invariably … calmer.

Your ancestors walked through all weathers, across all terrains. Your body still wants to move through the world – it doesn't care if it's dark. Give it what it wants.

5. Why nature works (and no, it's not just pretty trees)

You might have noticed that I keep talking about walking in the countryside – through fields, along lanes, across farmland. That's not nostalgia or aesthetic preference. There's a reason for it.

Walking in nature is demonstrably, measurably more effective for anxiety than walking in urban environments.

The science on this is unambiguous. In one well-known Stanford study, participants were assigned fifty-minute walks either in natural settings or in urban ones. The nature walkers showed reduced anxiety, less rumination (that grim, repetitive thinking anxiety thrives on) and improved working memory. The urban walkers? Not so much.

The Japanese have a practice called *shinrin-yoku*, which translates as 'forest bathing'. Despite how it sounds, it isn't mystical or performative. It simply involves being present in a forested environment.

Studies conducted across twenty-four forests in Japan found that forest exposure reduced heart rate, blood pressure and cortisol levels compared to urban settings. And it wasn't limited to walking –simply looking at natural scenes produced measurable benefits.

There's also evidence that trees release chemicals called phytoncides – volatile organic compounds that appear to have direct anti-anxiety and anti-inflammatory effects when inhaled. Your brain evolved surrounded by trees. It knows them. It relaxes around them.

This isn't spiritual mumbo-jumbo. It's evolutionary biology.

One large study found that people who regularly walked in green spaces had forty-three per cent fewer days of poor mental health than non-walkers. Another showed that as little as thirty minutes a week spent in outdoor green space reduced depression by 7 per cent. These aren't marginal effects. This is free, readily available medicine sitting just outside your door.

Now, I know not everyone lives in the countryside. Maybe you're reading this in a flat in Manchester or a terrace in London, and the nearest 'nature' is a scrappy park with more dog turds than trees. Here's the good news: even that helps.

Urban green spaces – parks, gardens, canal paths with a bit of overgrown vegetation – still calm the nervous system. Your brain isn't picky. It just wants something that isn't concrete, traffic and screens.

6. The walk at 3 am (or: when you can't sleep, don't lie there)

I should tell you about the time I went for a walk at 3 am. This is not normal behaviour, and I'm aware of that. But anxiety doesn't give a toss about what's normal.

It was a warm summer night, and I'd been lying awake since about 1 am with that particular flavour of anxiety that feels like electricity under your skin. You know the one – exhausted but wired, every position uncomfortable, thoughts looping endlessly.

For years, my strategy had been to lie there and fight it. I'd try to relax, tell myself to calm down and grow increasingly frustrated that I wasn't sleeping. Which, of course, made me more anxious and made sleep even more impossible. The classic anxious-insomnia death spiral.

But that night, something snapped. I thought, Fuck it. If I'm going to be awake, I might as well be awake outside.

I got dressed quietly so as not to wake anyone and stepped out into the night. It was extraordinary. The village was completely silent –no cars, no voices, not even a dog barking. The sky was that deep summer blue that isn't quite black, and the stars were out. The kind you forget exist when you live with light pollution.

I walked up the lane, past the church, and out into the fields where the wheat was nearly ready for harvest.

The anxiety was still there – but it felt different. Smaller. There's something about moving through an empty landscape at 3 am that puts your personal problems into perspective. The world doesn't care about your anxiety. The wheat doesn't care. The stars don't care. And somehow, that isn't depressing … it's liberating.

I walked for about forty-five minutes. By the time I got home, I was physically tired in a way I hadn't been before – the good kind of tired that comes from moving your body, not lying still and thinking. I got back into bed and fell asleep almost immediately.

I'm not suggesting everyone start wandering around at 3 am. There are safety considerations, and your neighbours might think you've finally lost the plot. But if you're lying awake fighting anxiety, maybe stop fighting.

Maybe get up.

Maybe move.

7. The counter-intuitive truth about movement and anxiety

Here's something that took me years to understand anxious people often avoid exercise not because they're lazy, but because the physical sensations of exercise – an increased heart rate, breathlessness, sweating – feel exactly like the sensations of panic.

Evolutionarily, this makes perfect sense. Your body can't tell the difference between heart racing because I'm running and heart racing because there's a threat. It just knows heart racing. And if you've trained yourself to fear that sensation – as most anxious people have – then exercise itself starts to feel dangerous.

Psychologists call this anxiety sensitivity: the tendency to misinterpret and catastrophise anxiety-related bodily sensations. And here's the crucial part – studies show that regular exercise reduces anxiety sensitivity.

Why? Because when you repeatedly experience an elevated heart rate in a genuinely safe context, your brain learns something new. It learns that a pounding heart isn't a signal of danger. In effect, you're doing exposure therapy for your own body.

This is why walking is such a good place to start. It raises your heart rate gently enough to retrain your nervous system, but not so much that it tips you into panic. It's exposure therapy in comfortable shoes.

I remember the first time I noticed this shift. I was walking up a steep hill, heart pounding, lungs working hard, and a familiar alarm went off in my head: Heart racing. Something's wrong. Danger.

But another voice – quieter, newer, built by months of regular walking – answered back: No, mate. That's just a hill. You're fine.

And I was fine. Better than fine. I was climbing a hill in the English countryside, my heart doing exactly what hearts are meant to do. Nothing was wrong. I was just alive.

8. How to actually do this (without making it another thing to fail at)

I know how anxious people think because I am one. By now, you're already lining up the reasons this won't work for you:

- 'I don't have time'
- 'I don't live near the countryside'
- 'I'll look stupid walking by myself'
- 'What if I have a panic attack outside?'

So let me deal with these, one by one, with the loving bluntness of someone who has used every excuse on that list.

'I don't have time.'

Even ten minutes of walking has measurable effects on anxiety. You spend longer than that scrolling on your phone on the toilet. Wake up ten minutes earlier. Walk for ten minutes at lunch. Get off the bus a stop early. You don't lack time – you're choosing how to use it.

'I don't live near the countryside.'

Any green space helps: a park, a garden, a canal path, a tree-lined street. And even without greenery, walking still works. The bilateral movement still calms the nervous system. Endorphins still flow. Cortisol still drops. Nature amplifies the benefits, but it isn't a requirement.

'I'll look stupid walking by myself.'

No one is watching you. They're far too busy worrying about themselves. And if they do notice, the thought is simply: There goes someone walking. That's it. No judgement. No commentary. Just a human moving through space, as humans have done for the last two million years.

'What if I have a panic attack outside?'

Then you have a panic attack outside. You won't die. You might feel embarrassed. And then it will pass – just like it would have indoors. I've had panic attacks on walks. I've sat on stiles hyperventilating. I've leaned against trees waiting for my heart to slow down. And then I've kept walking. Because that's what you do.

9. Adam's walking practice

Here's what works for me. Take what's useful. Ignore the rest.

Daily minimum:

Twenty minutes of walking, no matter what. Cold, dark, tired – it doesn't matter. It's twenty minutes, it's non-negotiable and it's baseline maintenance, like brushing my teeth. I don't debate it. I don't negotiate with my mood. I just go.

When anxiety is high:
Longer walks. At least forty-five minutes. The first twenty minutes are usually for getting past the worst of it. The next twenty-five are where the real shift happens.

Winter evenings:
Head torch on. Fields behind my house. Cold air, darkness, silence. Some of my most calming walks have happened in conditions that would have terrified the old me. Turns out the things I avoided were often the things that helped most.

The rule:
I don't try to use walking to fix anxiety. I walk with anxiety. There's a difference.

If I walk trying to make anxiety go away, I'm still fighting it. But if I walk alongside it – two companions travelling the same path – something shifts. The struggle drops. The grip loosens.

No headphones:
This one's personal, but my walks are more effective without podcasts or music. The point isn't distraction; it's presence. Let the mind wander. Let the thoughts come. Keep walking anyway.

10. The walk that's waiting

That walk I described on the hillside – the one where I laughed because I finally understood something – wasn't a miracle cure. The anxiety came back. It always does.

But something fundamental had changed. I'd walked through anxiety instead of running from it. I'd learned that I could be anxious and still be okay. That moving my body through the world – one foot in front of the other – was one of the most powerful tools I had.

Your body was built to walk. For two million years, your ancestors walked across savannahs, through forests, over mountains. They walked to find food, escape danger and reach new ground. Walking isn't exercise – it's what you are. It's written into you.

And right now, wherever you are, there's a walk waiting.

Maybe it's a path through local fields.

Maybe it's a loop around the park.

Maybe it's just up and down your street until you've clocked twenty minutes.

It doesn't matter where. What matters is that you go.

Put this book down. Put your shoes on. Go outside. And if it's dark, strap on a head torch and go anyway. Your pink spaghetti mistress can come if she wants – but she'll get tired before you do.

CHAPTER SIXTEEN

THE ART OF SELF-SABOTAGE

'My anxiety once whispered I was about to die. Turns out I just needed to pee and drink some water.' – Adam Knights

Last Thursday, I ate an entire packet of chocolate digestives over the course of an hour. I followed that with a huge kebab, three whiskeys and then a fourth whiskey, because the third one looked lonely.

Did I need any of this? No.

Was I hungry? Not remotely.

Did I know, with absolute clarity, that I was sabotaging myself?

Of course I bloody did – and I did it anyway.

Here's the thing no one tells you about anxiety: even when you've made friends with it, even when you've learned to understand it and live alongside it, there will still be days when you actively work against yourself. Days when you reach for the very thing you know will make it worse – precisely because it will make it worse.

THE ONE IN A HUNDRED MILLION: A MASTER-CLASS IN CATASTROPHISING

Let me tell you about the time I caught HIV from a sneeze.

I didn't, obviously. But for two weeks, my anxiety had me absolutely convinced that I was the one person in human history to contract the virus through airborne transmission. I was the unluckiest man alive.

This, my fellow sufferers, is catastrophising and it is the beating heart of my anxiety. It's the engine that powers the whole bloody machine.

THE SNEEZE THAT LAUNCHED A THOUSAND TERRORS

I was in Mumbai, doing what I try to do on most trips (look out virtue signalling coming!) helping with food and water distribution for people living on the streets. I was handing out supplies, feeling moderately useful, when one of the people I was helping coughed and sneezed directly into my face.

They also had visible open sores on their body.

The kind of visible sores your brain quietly files away for later use.

I barely registered it at the time. I was busy. There were hundreds of people to help. I wiped my face, carried on and didn't think about it again.

That's the thing about catastrophising – it rarely happens in real time. Your anxious brain needs a quiet moment to really get to work. It isn't interested in bothering you while you're doing something useful. It waits patiently, like a cat waiting for you to settle on the sofa before depositing a dead mouse on your lap.

Three days later, I got properly ill. Flu-like symptoms: body aches, exhaustion, the full miserable package.

My anxiety took one look at the timing and said,

'Interesting.'

THE CREDENTIALS THAT MEAN NOTHING

I should mention at this point that I've worked in healthcare for nearly twenty-five years. I know how HIV transmission works. I've read the literature. I've attended the conferences. I know – with professional, evidence-based certainty – that you cannot catch HIV from a sneeze.

You. Cannot. Catch. HIV. From. A. Sneeze.

The virus doesn't survive in saliva or in air. It requires very specific kinds of direct blood-to-blood or bodily fluid contact. I could give you a thirty-minute presentation on the subject, complete with PowerPoint slides and peer-reviewed sources.

But anxiety doesn't care about your credentials.

She isn't interested in your qualifications, your decades of experience or your ability to cite epidemiological data. She's interested in the what if.

'What if you're the one in a hundred million?' she whispers.

'What if you're the exception?'

'What if this is the first documented case and you're about to become a medical anomaly – studied in journals and cited in textbooks?'

'Patient Zero for Airborne HIV: The Adam Jenkins Case.'

And just like that, I'm convinced I'm dying.

WHAT YOUR BRAIN IS ACTUALLY DOING

Let me explain what's happening neurologically when you catastrophise because understanding this helped me enormously. It didn't stop me doing it – but it helped me recognise it for what it was.

Your brain has two key players in this drama.

In the red corner, we have the amygdala – the almond-shaped fear centre deep in your temporal lobe. It's ancient and primal, evolved to keep your ancestors alive on the savannah by assuming every rustle in the grass was a lion. It doesn't do nuance or probability calculations, but it does do:

THREAT. RESPOND. NOW.

In the blue corner, we have the prefrontal cortex: the rational, thinking part of your brain. It's the newer model, evolved more recently, and it handles logic, reason, planning and the ability to say, 'Hang on, let's think about this properly.'

When you're not anxious, these two systems work

together. The amygdala spots something potentially concerning and sends up a flag. The prefrontal cortex evaluates it: That rustling? Just the wind. Stand down. It's civilised. Cooperative. Effective.

But when you're catastrophising, that communication breaks down completely. The amygdala becomes hyperactive, while the prefrontal cortex gets suppressed. Research shows that during catastrophic thinking the amygdala works overtime while activity in the prefrontal cortex decreases. You are literally becoming less capable of rational thought at exactly the moment you need it most.

It's like having a fire alarm that's hypersensitive to burnt toast –except every time it goes off, it also disconnects the sprinkler system. Brilliant design, evolution. Really excellent work.

THE CATASTROPHISING LOOP (OR HOW TO MAKE YOURSELF WORSE)

Here's where it gets fun. Catastrophising creates a feedback loop that makes everything worse.

The thought I might have HIV triggers the amygdala. The amygdala floods the body with stress hormones like adrenaline and cortisol. Those hormones produce physical symptoms: racing heart, tight chest, nausea, muscle tension, difficulty concentrating.

And what does the anxious brain do with those symptoms?

It treats them as evidence.

See? You feel terrible. Something's wrong. Your body knows.

The anxiety creates symptoms that feel like proof of the thing you're anxious about. That 'proof' increases the anxiety, which creates more symptoms, which feel like more proof. It's a self-sustaining loop of dread.

I spent two weeks stuck inside it. Two weeks monitoring my body for symptoms. Two weeks of Googling early HIV signs (never, ever do this). Two weeks lying awake at night replaying the sneeze, the open sores, the possibility of a microscopic droplet of blood. Maybe I'd had a tiny cut on my face. Maybe the virus had somehow made it through.

Occasionally, my prefrontal cortex would try to intervene.

'Adam, you literally know this is impossible. You have

decades of professional knowledge about this exact subject.'

And the amygdala would reply:

'But what if you're wrong? What if everything you know is wrong – and what if this is the one time?'

The amygdala always wins in the short term. That's the nature of the beast.

THE ONE-IN-A-HUNDRED-MILLION PROBLEM

Catastrophising has a peculiar relationship with probability – one I find darkly fascinating.

Under normal circumstances, humans weigh likelihood. If something has a one-in-a-million chance of happening, we treat it as effectively impossible and get on with our lives. We don't avoid going outside because meteorites kill about one person a year. We don't refuse to eat because food can, technically, cause anaphylactic shock.

Catastrophic thinking works differently. It treats low-probability negative outcomes as certainties, while simultaneously ignoring high-probability neutral or positive ones.

My brain was utterly convinced I was the medical anomaly who'd caught HIV from a sneeze – a probability so low it might as well be zero. Yet that same brain couldn't accept the virtually certain explanation that I'd simply caught a cold or flu, like millions of people do every day.

Why?

Because the catastrophic outcome is emotionally

compelling. The amygdala doesn't do maths; it does threat assessment. If you have a common cold it doesn't register as a problem worth attention. If you have a fatal disease it absolutely does.

Researchers call this probability neglect: the tendency to ignore actual likelihood when an outcome carries a strong emotional charge. It's why people fear plane crashes more than car crashes, despite cars being statistically far more dangerous. It's why terrorism feels more threatening than heart disease.

And it's why I spent two weeks convinced I was dying from an impossibility, while completely discounting the boring, mundane and overwhelmingly likely explanation.

DR GOOGLE WILL SEE YOU NOW (AND HE HAS TERRIBLE NEWS)

I should tell you about the Googling. Because I know you've done it too.

At 1 am, lying in bed, wide awake and wired, I did what every catastrophising anxious person eventually does: I reached for my phone and typed 'HIV transmission methods' into Google.

This is, objectively, insane behaviour.

I already knew the answer. I'd known the answer for decades. But the anxious brain doesn't want knowledge; it wants reassurance –and it wants it the way an addict wants a fix. Google is always there, glowing gently in the dark, ready to offer just one more hit of information that will surely be the one that finally puts the fear to rest.

Except it never works like that.

Reassurance-seeking is a trap. Each piece of information provides a brief flicker of relief, immediately followed by: 'Yes, but what about …' And down the rabbit hole you go.

Here's how my 2 am Google session played out:

- **Search:** HIV transmission methods
- **Result:** HIV is transmitted through blood, sexual fluids and breast milk. Not saliva. Not sneezes.
- **Brain:** Good. That's reassuring. But what if there was blood in the sneeze?
- **Search:** Can HIV be transmitted through blood in a sneeze?
- **Result:** No documented cases. The virus doesn't survive in air.
- **Brain:** Yes, but 'no documented cases' just means it hasn't been observed yet. What if I'm the first?
- **Search:** HIV survival outside the body
- **Result:** HIV is fragile outside the body. Dies within seconds to minutes in open air.
- **Brain:** But what if it survived just long enough? What if the sneeze was particularly … moist?

And so it went on. For hours.

Every answer was interrogated, found wanting and replaced with another what if. The more I searched, the worse I felt. Each reassurance was immediately undermined by the next catastrophic thought, like a game of psychological whack-a-mole where the mallet is broken and the moles are armed.

This is why health professionals tell people with anxiety to stop Googling symptoms. Not because the information is inaccurate – but because the anxious brain will always find a way to weaponise accurate information against you.

It's incredibly creative like that.

THE TEST (OR PAYING MONEY TO CONFIRM WHAT I ALREADY KNEW)

After two weeks of this nonsense, I did what any self-respecting hypochondriac does: I got tested.

Not because I genuinely believed I had HIV. Even in my most catastrophic moments, there was always a part of me – the professional, the rational adult who's spent his career in healthcare – that knew this was absurd. I got tested because I needed external validation. I needed something tangible to wave at my anxious brain.

'Look. Here. A piece of paper. Negative. Now will you shut up?'

The results came back clean. No HIV. No hepatitis. Nothing remarkable at all, except a slightly elevated white cell count consistent with … wait for it … a recent viral infection.

I'd had the flu.

The relief was extraordinary.

For about three hours.

Because here's the thing about reassurance-seeking: it works briefly, and then it fails completely. The anxious brain builds tolerance. The reassurance that calmed you yesterday calms you a little less today, and tomorrow it won't work at all.

Within a day, my brain was already questioning the results.

'What if it was too early to detect?'

'What if the test missed it?'

'What if you should get tested again in three months, just to be sure?'

This is the treadmill of health anxiety. You can never run fast enough to get off it. Every reassurance creates the need for more reassurance. Every test invites another test. Every clear result is immediately suspect.

THE GREATEST HITS ALBUM

I wish I could tell you that the HIV-sneeze episode was a one-off – a moment of unusual weakness I learned from and never repeated.

It wasn't.

Over the years, I've been convinced I was dying from an impressive catalogue of conditions. Here's a partial list, because if I can't laugh at myself, what's the point:

- **Brain tumour:** A headache for three days. Obviously cancer.

(It was eye strain from staring at a computer screen.)

- **Heart attack:** Chest pain, left-arm tingling. Classic signs. Called an ambulance. Twice.

(Anxiety-induced muscle tension. Both times.)

- **Bowel cancer:** Changes in bowel habits. Googled it. Six months to live.

(It was the curry I'd had the night before.)

- **Multiple sclerosis:** Numbness in my legs. Neurological deterioration.

(I'd been sitting cross-legged too long and cut off the circulation.)

- **Throat cancer:** Persistent sore throat. Had to be malignant.

(Post-nasal drip from hay fever.)

- **ALS:** Muscle twitching. Motor neurone disease. (Too much coffee.)
- **Rabies:** Licked by a stray dog in Manila. Missed the jab window. Certainly fatal.

(The dog was healthy. I was fine. Still am.)

EACH OF THESE EPISODES FOLLOWED THE SAME BASIC PATTERN

- A normal body sensation or minor symptom
- A catastrophic interpretation
- Anxiety – followed by physical symptoms caused by the anxiety itself
- Those symptoms being read as confirmation of illness. More anxiety. Google. Even more anxiety

- Reassurance-seeking. Brief relief. Anxiety returns
- Eventual resolution – either through time, testing or the arrival of a new health worry that quietly replaces the old one.

It's genuinely, bone-achingly exhausting.

The mental energy required to maintain several simultaneous death scenarios is extraordinary.

If I could have channelled that creativity and attention to detail into literally anything else, I'd probably have written several novels and cured a disease by now.

THE HYPERVIGILANCE PROBLEM (OR PAYING FAR TOO MUCH ATTENTION TO YOUR OWN BODY)

Here's something I learned that actually helped: people with health anxiety pay far more attention to their bodies than other people do – and not in a healthy way.

Your body is doing strange, harmless things all the time. Muscles twitch. Hearts skip beats. Digestion gurgles. Random pains appear and disappear without explanation.

Most people don't notice any of this because their brains filter it out as unimportant background noise. The anxious brain doesn't. It's hypervigilant – constantly scanning for threats, including internal ones – and every minor sensation gets flagged, examined and catastrophically interpreted.

The cruel irony is that hypervigilance creates symptoms.

When you pay intense attention to your heart, you become aware of every beat and every tiny irregularity.

When you monitor your breathing, you start breathing oddly – which makes you more aware of your breathing – which makes you breathe even more oddly. The act of looking for problems creates the experience of problems.

I spent years doing this. Constantly scanning. Constantly questioning.

Was that pain normal? Was that twitch there yesterday? Why does my heartbeat feel different? Why is my vision slightly blurry? What is that weird sensation in my stomach?

The answer, almost always, was simple: it's normal. You're just paying attention.

But what if this time it wasn't normal?

And what if this was the one that mattered?

THE THING THAT ACTUALLY HELPED

So what changed? How did I go from convincing myself I was dying every other week to still occasionally convincing myself I'm dying, but far less often and with much less conviction?

It wasn't a single breakthrough or sudden moment of clarity. It was a gradual shift in how I related to catastrophic thoughts.

My old approach was to fight them. To argue. To prove them wrong with evidence and logic.

'No, brain, you're wrong. Here's why you're wrong. Here's the evidence that you're wrong. Please stop being wrong.'

This, unsurprisingly, doesn't work. You can't argue with an amygdala. It doesn't speak the same language. The more you engage with catastrophic thoughts, the more real they become and every argument reinforces their importance.

The new approach – the one I learned when I stopped fighting my anxiety and started dating her instead – was very different.

'Oh, there you are. I see you're doing the catastrophising thing again. That's interesting. Carry on.'

It wasn't fighting or agreeing. It was noticing, acknowledging and then getting on with whatever I was doing.

This sounds unbearably simple, and in some ways it is. But it's also incredibly difficult. The urge to engage, to argue, to seek reassurance, to Google and to get tested is overwhelming.

Letting catastrophic thoughts be there without doing anything about them requires a kind of radical acceptance that goes against every instinct.

But here's the thing: catastrophic thoughts are like fire. They need fuel to keep burning. Engagement – whether it's arguing against them, seeking reassurance or Googling symptoms – is that fuel. When you stop engaging, you stop feeding them and eventually, starved of attention, they die down.

They don't disappear. My brain still occasionally tries to convince me I'm dying.

Just last month I had a brief but intense conviction that a mole on my arm was melanoma. (It wasn't. It's been there for twenty-five years.) But now I recognise the pattern. I notice the thought. I feel the familiar pull towards catastrophe.

'Hello, old friend. I see what you're doing. I'm not going to play today.'

And most of the time – not always, but most of the time – it works.

CHAPTER SEVENTEEN

WE'RE ALL THE ONE IN A HUNDRED MILLION

'Living with anxiety is like sharing a flat with someone who criticises everything you do, but occasionally saves your life.'
– Adam Knights

Here's the thing my anxiety got right, even while getting almost everything else wrong: we are all the one in a hundred million.

The probability of you – your exact genetic makeup, consciousness and lived experience – existing at all is so vanishingly small it's effectively zero. The chain of events required for you to be here is absurdly long and fragile: your parents meeting, their parents meeting, every ancestor stretching back millions of years surviving long enough to reproduce, and every random genetic combination landing exactly right.

Miss one step. One conversation. One illness. One

accident. And you're not here.

You are already the impossible outcome. The medical anomaly. The one-in-a-hundred-million event that has already happened. It's called being alive.

So yes, I am the one in a hundred million – just not in the way my anxiety feared. And so are you.

- You're not going to be the first person to catch HIV from a sneeze.
- You're not going to be the exception to every medical probability.
- Your headache is almost certainly not a brain tumour.
- Your chest pain is almost certainly not a heart attack, and that weird feeling in your stomach is almost certainly the dodgy prawn sandwich you had for lunch.
- But you are a miraculous, impossible, one-in-a-hundred-million event. You're just not dying from it. At least, not today. Probably. (Sorry. Old habits.)

THE EXPERT INDUSTRIAL COMPLEX (OR HOW I LEARNED TO STOP WORRYING AND TRUST MYSELF)

'An expert is anybody who is more than fifty miles from home.'
– Mark Twain

Mark Twain, in my view, was one of the finest writers who ever lived. He's up there with Orwell in wit, clarity and the ability to cut through nonsense with a single sentence. Both men had an uncanny talent for exposing the gap between what people say they're doing and what they're actually doing.

Orwell did it with politics; Twain did it with everything else. And on the subject of experts, Twain nailed it over a century ago. Though if he were alive today, I suspect he'd amend it to: 'An expert is anybody with a LinkedIn profile and a podcast.'

Here's the thing about anxiety that the wellness industry doesn't want you to know – because if you knew it, they'd have to find real jobs: **you are the expert**. You. The person reading this at 3 am because your pink spaghetti mistress decided now would be a perfect time to replay every awkward conversation you've ever had.

You are the one who has spent decades learning the language of your own nervous system, who knows exactly which triggers send you spiralling and which coping mechanisms actually work.

Not some well-meaning therapist who did a weekend certification in 'Anxiety Management for Wellness Practitioners'. Not the life coach who discovered their calling after a transformative yoga retreat in Bali. Not the author of *Heal Your Anxiety in 30 Days: The Ultimate Guide to Inner Peace,* who has never felt their heart try to escape through their throat because they couldn't remember if they locked the front door.

You.

FOLLOW THE MONEY (BECAUSE IT'S A BLOODY FORTUNE)

Before you dismiss me as some bitter old soldier who doesn't understand the value of professional mental health support, consider the numbers – they're enough to make your anxiety spike … and this time, justifiably.

The global mental wellness market was valued at approximately **$166 billion in 2024.** By 2032, it's projected to reach nearly **$300 billion.** That's not a typo. Three hundred billion dollars. That's not healthcare – it's an industry. Bigger than the GDP of many countries. Enough to create 'experts' out of thin air because there's gold in those anxious hills.

In the United States alone, the behavioural health market hit **$87.82 billion in 2024**, while the broader 'mental wellness' sector, which includes therapy, meditation apps and brain-boosting supplements, clocked in at **$73.3 billion.**

And here's the kicker: the global wellness economy reached **$6.3 trillion in 2023.** To put that in perspective, it's larger than the pharmaceutical industry, larger than the global IT sector and roughly 60 per cent the size of all global health expenditure combined.

Now, I'm not naturally suspicious – actually, that's bollocks, I am deeply suspicious, and it's kept me alive in Belfast – but when I see an industry growing at 7 per cent annually while actual human well-being metrics decline, I start asking questions.

THE GREAT DISORDER EXPANSION

Let me tell you a story about a book. Not a very exciting book, mind you – its clinical prose makes Swedish furniture instruction manuals seem riveting. Yet this book has probably shaped how we think about our minds more than any religious text or philosophical treatise.

The Diagnostic and Statistical Manual of Mental Disorders (DSM) is psychiatry's Bible. It tells clinicians what to call the things that go wrong in people's heads – and, just as importantly for our purposes, it tells insurance companies what they'll pay for.

When the first edition was published in 1952, it was 130 pages long and listed **106 mental disorders** – 106 ways for the human mind to malfunction. It seemed thorough at the time.

By 1980, the ***DSM-III*** had ballooned to 886 pages and 265 disorders. In just 28 years, the human mind had apparently discovered many new and innovative ways to break down.

The ***DSM-IV-TR*** in 2000 listed 365 disorders, and the current ***DSM-5-TR*** includes around 297 distinct diagnoses, with over 70 modifications made since 2013.

Among the newer additions is **Prolonged Grief Disorder** – because apparently, grieving 'too long' is now a medical condition requiring professional intervention. Pause and consider that: grieving is one of the most fundamentally human experiences, a natural response to losing someone we love. And now, it's pathologised and billable.

As one psychiatrist admitted rather candidly, the *DSM*, through copyrights held by the American Psychiatric Association, has earned the organisation over **$100 million.** Not bad for a book that essentially invents the conditions it claims to diagnose.

THE MODERN ALPHABET SOUP OF SUFFERING

Let's look at some conditions that didn't exist – or at least weren't considered disorders – when I had my first panic attack during weapons training in the 1980s. Back then, I was told to 'man up' and 'get on with it'. It wasn't helpful, but at least it was free.

- **Social communication disorder:** Added in *DSM-5*. If you're awkward at parties and struggle with small talk, congratulations – you may have a disorder. (Or you might just be British.)
- **Disruptive mood dysregulation disorder:** Also in *DSM-5*, for children with severe temper tantrums. My generation called these 'difficult phases' and treated them with the revolutionary intervention of growing out of it.
- **Hoarding disorder:** Split from OCD in *DSM-5*. My grandmother kept everything from the war; we called her 'resourceful'. Now she'd have a diagnosis and a treatment plan.
- **Binge eating disorder:** *DSM-5* gave this full disorder status – because eating too much cake on a bad day

is apparently a mental illness. (Sometimes it's just Tuesday.)

- **Internet gaming disorder:** Proposed for further study. Playing too many video games is now 'almost' a disorder.
- **Caffeine withdrawal:** Your morning headache when you skip coffee? Potentially billable.
- **Premenstrual dysphoric disorder:** Because being a woman with a menstrual cycle is apparently a mental health condition requiring professional management.
- **Prolonged grief disorder:** My personal favourite, added in 2022. If you're still grieving 'too much' a year after losing someone you love, congratulations – you have a disorder. Recommended treatment? Six to sixteen sessions of cognitive behavioural therapy at £100–200 per session. Up to £3,200 to be taught how to grieve 'properly'.

Now, let me be clear: **I am not dismissing genuine mental illness.** Schizophrenia is real and my beloved aunty has it. Bipolar disorder is real. Severe clinical depression that leaves you unable to get out of bed is terrifyingly, devastatingly real. These conditions require professional help, medication and often hospitalisation.

But there's a difference between those and 'you're a bit sad because life is difficult'. There's a difference between a brain that's genuinely malfunctioning and a mind that's responding entirely appropriately to an insane world. The former needs treatment. The latter? A good friend, a stiff drink and possibly a different job.

THE ADHD EXPLOSION: A CASE STUDY

Let me illustrate this with ADHD, because the numbers are striking, and because I've personally run into this corner of the industry.

ADHD first appeared in the DSM in 1968 as **'Hyperkinetic Reaction of Childhood'.** Sounds like something a child catches from a particularly enthusiastic trampoline session.

Since then, the condition has been renamed, redefined and expanded with each subsequent edition. *DSM-5* in 2013 made several major changes:

- Raised the age of onset from 7 to 12
- Reduced the number of symptoms needed for an adult diagnosis
- Crucially, removed the exclusion preventing a person from being diagnosed with both ADHD and autism.

That last change alone added a massive population of potential patients who were previously excluded.

The result? ADHD diagnoses have skyrocketed in groups that were previously underdiagnosed – women, minorities, adults. Rates have increased three to four times in just two decades. Some of this reflects genuine recognition of previously overlooked issues and does it exist? Yes of course. It is, however, just another label and I don't like labels.

A couple of years ago a friend of mine was told he had late-stage ADHD. Late stage – as if it was cancer, or as if his inability to focus during boring meetings were a terminal condition demanding urgent intervention.

The assessment? £3,000. Just for the privilege of being told what was supposedly wrong with him – not for treatment, medication or ongoing support. He could have bought a decent second-hand car for that. Instead, he was offered the chance to pay three grand to receive a label that didn't exist when he was a child and that, conveniently, seemed to require further costly treatment.

He declined. Somehow, he managed to muddle through life without that particular label, and I suspect he will continue to do so.

This pattern is being repeated across the diagnostic landscape. Autism spectrum disorder has expanded; anxiety disorders have proliferated into dozens of subspecies and depression has been sliced and diced into so many varieties that there's almost certainly one to fit whatever you're feeling right now. And every new disorder creates a need: experts to diagnose it, treatments to cure it, medications to manage it. Ka-ching.

THE PRICE OF CARING (SPOILER ALERT ...IT'S EXTORTIONATE)

I've watched intelligent, capable friends struggling to get help get absolutely ripped off by this industry.

One friend paid £700 for a single sixty-minute session with someone who had letters after their name, just to receive a diagnosis, not treatment.

£700 an hour. That's more than most barristers charge, more than many surgeons bill for life-saving procedures, and more than you'd pay a top-tier financial adviser who might actually make you money.

And here's the question I keep coming back to: if these people truly cared really, genuinely cared, wouldn't the costs be far lower?

Think about it. If you genuinely believed your work was helping people in desperate need, if you truly saw your role as healing the sick and comforting the distressed, would you charge the equivalent of a family holiday for a diagnosis? Would you erect financial barriers between suffering people and the help they need?

The NHS is overwhelmed; waiting lists stretch for months or years. Into that gap steps private practice, hand outstretched, demanding £700 for an hour of chat. And we're supposed to believe this is about caring? About helping? About the sacred Hippocratic principle of 'do no harm'? No.

The people charging these rates aren't driven by compassion –they're driven by the same forces that drive every other business: supply, demand and what the market will bear. And the market, unfortunately, is made up of desperate people who will pay almost anything to feel better.

That's not healthcare. That's exploitation with a therapy qualification.

PRIMUM NON NOCERE (FIRST, DO NO HARM)

Every doctor, at some point in their training, encounters the Latin phrase *primum non nocere* – 'first, do no harm'. It's the foundational principle of medicine, attributed to Hippocrates, though probably coined centuries later by Thomas Sydenham. The idea is simple: before you intervene, make sure you're not making things worse.

Somewhere along the line, I'd argue, the mental health industry lost sight of this principle – or more accurately, chose to ignore it. Harm prevention doesn't scale as well as treatment provision, and business models tend to reward intervention over restraint.

When you label a normal human response to a difficult life as a 'disorder', you are doing harm. You're telling someone they are broken, that resilience is pathology and that they cannot handle their own problems. You're handing authority over their mind to an external expert. That's not harmless ... it's harm.

Prescribing medication for every dip in mood, sleepless night or bout of nervousness creates both physiological and psychological dependency. It tells someone they cannot function without pharmaceutical intervention, potentially making them a patient for life. That's not harmless ... it's harm.

When an entire industry treats normal experiences – grief, anxiety, restlessness, sadness – as medical conditions requiring professional treatment, it's not just misguided; it's catastrophic. Society is taught that ordinary humans cannot navigate life without expert assistance. That's harm on a generational scale.

FINDING WHAT WORKS (THE HARD WAY)

Before you think I'm some anti-treatment zealot dismissing mental health support, let me share my journey. It illustrates exactly why you must find what works for you.

I've tried everything: breathing exercises, meditation apps, self-help books (enough to build a small extension), CBT, counselling, talking therapies and alternative approaches that seemed promising at 2 am and ridiculous by morning light. Most of it was useless. Some was actively counterproductive. And a fair bit simply separated me from money I could have spent on something that actually helped, like a decent whisky or a holiday somewhere warm.

But and this is crucial, I got lucky.

After years of trial and error of kissing therapeutic frogs, I found a psychologist who is genuinely exceptional. (Sorry Julie, I had to mention you!) She understands my specific brand of anxiety, doesn't try to fit me into a textbook framework, challenges me when I need challenging and supports me when I need supporting.

I also found a medication combination that works for

me – not perfectly, nothing ever is – but well enough that I can function, sleep and face the day without my chest tightening at the thought of what might go wrong.

Finding what works took years and patience I didn't know I had. I learned to accept that what works for someone else might not work for me, and that the experts' recommendations can sometimes be completely wrong for my particular nervous system.

The point isn't that professional help is worthless. It's that you have to find what works for you. That means trusting your experience, ignoring the experts when they're wrong and persisting when the first, or fifth or tenth approach fails.

Because the rare professionals who truly help will tell you the same thing: they're not there to fix you, they're there to help you figure out how to fix yourself.

THE REAL EXPERTS (HINT: IT'S NOT THEM)

Let me be clear: nuance matters here. This isn't a topic that benefits from absolutism. There are real experts – people whose skill and knowledge can be measured by tangible outcomes. Surgeons who spend fifteen years mastering how to repair a human heart without killing the patient. Neurologists who can read a brain scan and pinpoint the tumour causing your headaches. Psychiatrists who manage genuine psychotic breaks, where patients are a danger to themselves or others. These are experts.

They operate in a space governed by objective standards. When a surgeon operates, the patient either survives or doesn't. When a psychiatrist intervenes, the patient either stabilises or doesn't. Expertise here is measurable and accountable.

The vast majority of the mental wellness industry, however, does not operate in this space. Instead, it exists in the murky waters of subjective experience – where success is hard to measure and failure is easy to blame on the patient.

- A life coach charging £300 an hour to tell you to 'live your best life'? Not an expert.
- A wellness influencer selling 'mental clarity' supplements? Not an expert.
- A weekend-certified therapist exploring your 'inner child' for £150 a session? Not an expert.
- An app promising to cure anxiety through guided meditation for £12.99 a month? Not an expert.

The truth is **you are the real expert on your anxiety.**

You've been living with it for years, possibly decades. You know what triggers it, what worsens it and what provides relief. You can tell the difference between a panic attack and a heart attack (even if in the moment it feels otherwise). You recognise which thoughts are irrational, even when you can't stop thinking them.

No one has studied your anxiety longer than you have.

No one has more data on your specific experience. And no one has a greater stake in getting it right.

THE OCCASIONAL HELPFUL NUDGE

Does this mean you should never seek help? Of course not. Sometimes you need an outside perspective – especially when you've been so deep in your own head that you can't see the forest for the trees. Sometimes, a professional can offer a tool or technique you haven't tried yet.

The key word is **occasional**. It's a nudge, not a lifelong dependency. A consultation, not a subscription. A conversation with someone who might have useful insights – not a transfer of authority over your own mind to a 'qualified professional'.

In twenty-five years of living with anxiety, I've had perhaps half a dozen conversations with professionals that I would describe as genuinely helpful. Moments when someone said something that shifted my perspective or offered a technique I hadn't considered. My current psychologist accounts for several of those moments and that's why I keep seeing her. She's earned that trust.

The rest? Well-meaning people repeating advice you could find in books – or worse, offering actively harmful guidance because they have never experienced real anxiety. They operate from textbooks, not lived understanding.

The most useful thing anyone ever said to me about anxiety didn't come from a therapist at all – it came from a sergeant major in the Parachute Regiment. We were about to jump out of a perfectly functional aircraft, and I was experiencing what I now know was a panic attack but, at the time, just felt like dying.

He looked at me, saw exactly what was happening and said: 'Your body thinks you're going to die. You're not. Jump anyway. It'll figure out the difference eventually.'

That's not therapy. It's not a treatment plan. It's not evidence-based intervention. But it contained more practical wisdom about anxiety than a thousand self-help books: your body is lying to you; you can override it and the only way through is … through.

TAKING BACK YOUR MIND

I'm not writing this to be cruel or cynical, though I know it might be read that way. I'm writing it because I've watched a generation be taught that they are broken, that they cannot cope and that they need experts to navigate their own inner lives.

Meanwhile, a $300 billion industry grows fat on this learned helplessness, while actual mental health outcomes remain stagnant. More people are being treated for mental health conditions than ever before and yet more people report struggling with them. The more we medicalise human distress, the more distressed we seem to become. Are we getting better or worse after all this treatment?

Maybe the problem isn't that we need more experts.

Maybe the problem is that we've outsourced our well-being to an industry that profits from our continued unwellness.

Your anxiety is yours. It's part of you – not a disease to eradicate, but a relationship to manage. You are the foremost expert on yourself, with decades of experience, intimate knowledge of your mind and a profound investment in your own outcome.

The pink spaghetti mistress may be demanding, but she's your demanding mistress. Only you know how to keep her satisfied enough to get on with life.

So, by all means, seek the occasional helpful nudge. Read the books if they help. Try the techniques. See a professional if you genuinely hit a wall you can't climb alone. Be willing to kiss a lot of frogs until you find the rare ones who actually help.

But never, ever hand over the keys to your mind. Never believe that someone with a certificate knows you better than you know yourself. Never let a $300 billion industry convince you that you're too broken to function without their products or services. And for God's sake, never pay £3,000 for a diagnosis when you could buy a car.

You've survived this long. You've figured out more than you give yourself credit for. You've developed coping mechanisms that actually work for your brand of anxiety – even if they'd never make it into a clinical treatment manual.

You are the expert. Trust yourself.
Besides, if the experts really knew what they were doing, wouldn't we all be cured by now?

CHAPTER EIGHTEEN

ASKING YOUR ANXIETY FOR ADVICE

'Anxiety isn't something to conquer. It's something to cohabitate with.' – Adam Knights

Asking your anxiety for advice? I know what you're thinking ... finally, proof that I've completely lost the plot. Has this ex-paratrooper been inhaling too many fumes from his own nonsense?

Fair question. But before you close this book and use it as a very expensive coaster, hear me out, because this piece of madness might just be the sanest thing I've ever done.

Here's the situation: your anxiety isn't leaving. We've established that. So if this unwanted lodger is going to stick around anyway, we might as well make it useful.

Which brings me to a genuinely mental-sounding suggestion: ask your anxiety for its opinion. Before a challenging task – a speech, a pitch, a difficult conversation – sit down with your anxiety and have an actual consultation.

See, anxiety isn't entirely irrational. It's disproportionately rational. Think of it as a risk assessor on unlimited coffee whose job is to find problems. Most of what they find is nonsense, but buried in the frantic report is occasionally something genuinely worth addressing. The trick is learning to sift through the madness for the useful bits.

LIVING WITH YOUR ANXIOUS LOVER

(Or how I learned to stop worrying and accept that my brain is a dramatic arsehole)

So you've stopped fighting, you've started acknowledging and you've begun to accept. Now what? Now you learn to live with it.

I know that sounds like a cop-out. You've read this far hoping I'd reveal the secret exit, the hidden trapdoor, the magic combination of breathing exercises and positive affirmations that would finally, finally make this bloody thing go away. Sorry to disappoint, but there is no exit. There's only cohabitation.

Anxiety, in my experience, never fully leaves. It's part of how some brains are wired. Mine certainly is, and yours probably is too, or you wouldn't still be reading. But here's what took me twenty-five years to understand: living with anxiety is very different from being controlled by it. The anxiety stays, but your relationship with it changes. And that change is everything.

Think of it like a long-term relationship with a high-maintenance partner. Yes, they're going to have their moments. Yes, they'll need attention sometimes. And yes, there will be days when you wonder why you ever got involved.

You fantasise about a calmer partner – someone who doesn't wake you at 3 am to debate whether that mole on your back has changed shape, someone who can watch a news bulletin without triggering immediate calculations of your untimely death.

But there are good days too. Days when you barely notice them, when their quirks are almost endearing, when you catch yourself thinking: 'You know what? We make a pretty good team, you neurotic bastard.'

I've been in this relationship with my anxiety for years. We have an understanding: I don't try to kick it out, and it doesn't burn the house down … most of the time.

THE COHABITATION AGREEMENT

Living with anxiety is like having a flatmate convinced the building is always on fire. You can't make them leave – their name's on the lease, permanently, in ink that doesn't wash off. So you learn to work around them, develop systems, create boundaries and accept that every now and then, you're going to be woken at 2 am by someone standing over your bed asking if you remembered to turn off the oven.

My anxiety and I have developed what I call the cohabitation agreement. It's not written down – she'd only worry about the legal implications – but it goes something like this:

Her responsibilities:

- Alert me to genuine threats (rare, but occasionally useful)
- Provide endless creative material for catastrophic scenarios (less useful, but at least entertaining)
- Keep me humble by reminding me of every embarrassing thing I've ever done, usually at important moments
- Ensure I never, ever run out of things to worry about.

My responsibilities:

- Acknowledge her presence without letting her redecorate the entire house
- Not tell her to piss off (too often)
- Provide regular reassurance that we are not, in fact, dying
- Accept that some days she's going to be unbearable – and that's just how it is.

It's not a perfect arrangement. She violates the agreement constantly.

Just last week, she convinced me that a headache was a brain aneurysm, even though I'd had three glasses of wine the night before and the 'aneurysm' mysteriously disappeared after two paracetamol and a bacon sandwich.

But I violate the agreement too. I still occasionally tell her to shut up, which never works and always makes things worse.

The point isn't perfection. The point is that we're both still here, muddling through, neither of us having successfully murdered the other yet.

THE MORNING ROUTINE

Let me walk you through a typical morning in our shared existence.

6:47 am I wake up. Before I've even opened my eyes, she's there.

'You're awake. Good. We need to talk about that email you sent yesterday.'

'It's not even seven o'clock.'

'The one to the client. Third paragraph. You used "kind regards" instead of "best wishes". What do you think that signals?'

'That I was finishing an email?'

'It signals coldness. Distance. They're going to think you don't value the relationship. They might pull the contract. If they pull the contract, you'll lose the revenue. If you lose the revenue …'

'I'm going to make coffee now.'

'… you might have to sell the house. Have you thought about where you'd live? Because the rental market is brutal right now. Brutal.'

I get up and make coffee. She follows, naturally. She

always follows.

'Also, your chest feels a bit tight. Have you noticed that? I've noticed that.'

'I've been lying down for eight hours. Everything feels tight.'

'Could be cardiac. Just saying. Worth monitoring.'

I drink my coffee. She monitors my heartbeat. We both pretend this is normal.

By **7:30**, I'm in the shower and she's running through a mental inventory of everything that could go wrong today: the presentation that might bomb, the colleague who looked at me strangely yesterday, the weird sound the car made last week that I still haven't had checked, the fact that I haven't called my mother in three days and she's probably worried – or worse, offended.

'She's definitely offended. You should call her. But not now, because you'll be late. But if you don't call her soon ...'

'I'll call her at lunch.'

'Will you though? Will you really? Because you said that yesterday.'

I turn the shower to cold. Not because I'm a masochist – well, not entirely – but because it's the one thing that shuts her up. She hates the cold. For thirty seconds, while I'm gasping, swearing and questioning my life choices, there's blessed silence.

Then I get out, and she's waiting with a towel and fresh concerns.

'You should really get that mole checked.'

This is every single morning. Some mornings she's louder, some mornings she's quieter, but she's always there – the paranoid flatmate who never sleeps, never takes a day off and never lets me enjoy my bloody coffee in peace.

THE SOCIAL CALENDAR

Anxiety affects every aspect of life, but she has a special enthusiasm for social situations. If I have an event coming up, – a dinner, a party or a work function – she starts preparing roughly six weeks in advance.

'So, the Henderson party. Let's talk about it.'

'It's in October. It's August.'

'Exactly. We're behind schedule. What are you going to wear?'

'I haven't thought about it.'

'Well, you should. You need the right balance – smart enough to look like you've tried, casual enough not to look like you're trying too hard. What if you overdress? What if everyone else is in jeans and you turn up in a suit? They'll think you're a banker. Or worse, an estate agent.'

'I'll figure it out closer to the time.'

'And what will you talk about? Safe topics only. Nothing political, remember the Wilsons' barbecue. Nothing about work – you'll bore them. Nothing about your health – you'll sound like a hypochondriac.'

'I am a hypochondriac.'

'Yes, but they don't need to know that. Also, we need an exit strategy. If you feel overwhelmed, what's your excuse? You can't use "early meeting" again – they'll think you hate them.'

'Maybe I do hate them.'

'Don't be ridiculous. You don't hate them. You hate social interaction. Big difference. Now, the drive. What if there's traffic? Leave early, but not too early – you don't want to be the first one there. That's worse than being late. Much worse.'

This rehearsal continues for weeks. By the time the event arrives, I've gone over it so many times that reality feels like a rerun of a show I've already watched. I know my talking points, my exit strategies and exactly how long I can sustain small talk before excusing myself to 'check my phone' in the toilet.

The event itself is usually fine, often even enjoyable. But my anxiety doesn't care about outcomes – she's already moved on to the post-event analysis.

'Why did you say that thing about the weather? Who talks about weather? You sounded like someone's elderly uncle.'

'Everyone talks about the weather. It's British. It's what we do.'

'And the bit where you laughed at that joke? Too loud. Everyone noticed.'

'No one noticed.'

'Jennifer noticed. I saw her look at you. A "why is he laughing so loud" look.'

'It was not.'

'We should probably never go to another social event again.'

THE HEALTH OBSESSION

If anxiety had a hobby, it would be medical diagnosis. She's not qualified – obviously, no training whatsoever – but that doesn't stop her from having very strong opinions about every twinge, ache or sensation in my body.

Headache? Could be a tumour. Chest pain? Cardiac. Stomach ache? Early stage cancer, almost certainly. Feeling tired? Could be diabetes – or anaemia – or chronic fatigue syndrome. Or all three simultaneously.

She's particularly fond of rare conditions. Common ailments don't interest her. If I mention my knee hurts, she's not satisfied with, 'Probably walked too much yesterday.' She wants something exotic, with a Latin name, that she can Google at 2 am.

'Have you heard of Ehlers-Danlos syndrome?'

'No, and I don't want to.'

'Hypermobile joints. Chronic pain. Very underdiagnosed. Your knee could be a symptom.'

'My knee is a symptom of being forty-seven and having sat incorrectly on the sofa.'

'That's what they all say … until it's too late.'

She keeps a mental catalogue of every health scare we've ever had: the Great Heart Attack Panic of 2019, the

Definitely-Cancer-But-Actually-A-Cyst incident of 2021 and the time I was convinced I had MS because my foot went numb after an hour on the sofa watching television.

'Remember when you thought you were having a stroke?' she asks, fondly, as if recalling a pleasant holiday.

'I had a migraine.'

'Yes, but at the time, we didn't know that. Exciting hours, weren't they? The ambulance, the tests and the very patient nurse who explained – twice – that you weren't dying.'

'I'd rather not remember.'

'I thought you handled it beautifully. Very dignified. Apart from the crying, of course.'

THE FINANCIAL WORRIES

Money is another of her favourite topics – specifically, its absence, the potential future absence and the elaborate scenarios in which I lose everything and end up living in a cardboard box.

'Have you checked your bank balance today?'

'Yes.'

'And?'

'It's fine.'

'Fine isn't good. Fine is one unexpected expense away from disaster. What if the boiler breaks? The car dies? A recession hits; you lose clients, can't pay the mortgage and must sell the house at a loss in a buyer's market?'

'Then I'll deal with it.'

'Will you though? Really? Because I've done the calculations. If you lose 40 per cent of your income for more than six months, we're in serious trouble. I've prepared a spreadsheet.'

'You've prepared a spreadsheet?'

'Colour-coded. Red is bad. There's a lot of red.'

Enough is a concept she doesn't understand. There's always something that could go wrong, some financial disaster lurking around the corner. If I won the lottery, she'd worry about the tax implications. If I found a suitcase full of cash, she'd panic about money laundering charges.

'What if it's marked? What if they trace it back to you? What if …'

'I haven't found a suitcase full of cash.'

'Not yet. But what if you do? We should have a plan."'

THE NIGHT SHIFT

Daytime anxiety is one thing. You're busy, distracted, juggling tasks, people and coffee. Anxiety has to compete with actual life – and sometimes life wins.

But nighttime? Nighttime is her domain. There's something about 3 a.m that brings out her finest work. The house is quiet, distractions vanish and it's just you, the darkness and her infinite capacity for creative catastrophe.

'You awake?'

'I am now.'

'Good. Let's talk about climate change.'

'Let's not.'

'Or that comment you made at work eight years ago – the one that sounded fine at the time but was probably offensive. Remember that?'

'Vaguely.'

'Let's go through it word by word. I've prepared notes.'

The night shift is when she truly excels. During the day, her worries are simple: health, money, social faux pas. But at night, she expands into existential territory.

- What's the point of anything?
- What happens when you die?
- What if you've wasted your entire life?
- What if everyone secretly hates you and is just being polite?

'Have you considered that all your friendships might be based on mutual convenience rather than genuine affection?'

'I hadn't, but thanks for that.'

'When was the last time someone contacted you first – not to ask for something, just to talk?'

'I don't know. Recently?'

'Define "recently".'

'Can we please just go back to sleep?'

'Sleep is for people who don't have things to worry about. We are not those people.'

THE GOOD DAYS

Here's the thing: there are good days. Days when she's quiet, barely a whisper and I almost forget she's there. These days don't arrive because I've done something right, and they're not a reward for good behaviour … they just happen. The chemistry shifts, the clouds part and for a few hours, sometimes a whole day, I get to experience what I imagine 'normal' people feel like all the time.

On good days, I can drink coffee without checking my heart rate, send emails without proofreading them twelve times, have conversations without mentally reviewing every word afterward –and simply ... be.

'Nice day,' she eventually says, almost sulkily.

'Yes. It is.'

'Enjoy it while it lasts.'

'I intend to.'

'I'll be back.'

'I know.'

And she will be back because she always does. But these good days remind me why I keep going. They're proof the relationship isn't all bad, and that beneath the constant worry, the midnight catastrophes and the obsessive health monitoring, there's something almost functional here.

We have good days and bad days. Days that start bad and get better. Days that start good and fall apart. And days so thoroughly mediocre that neither of us can be bothered to comment.

That's the relationship. That's cohabitation. And that's what living with anxiety looks like once you stop trying to win and start learning to manage.

THE UNEXPECTED BENEFITS

I know this might sound insane, but sometimes anxiety is actually useful.

I can hardly believe I'm writing it, but it's true. Because she's constantly scanning for threats, I'm rarely caught off guard. I've planned for most disasters before they happen, and I've even got backup plans for my backup plans.

People come to me when things go wrong because I've already imagined every possible scenario and worked out contingencies.

'See?' she says smugly when my over-preparation pays off. 'Told you we needed to worry about that.'

'You told me to worry about seventeen things. Sixteen didn't happen.'

'But one did. And we were ready.'

She has a point. An annoying point, but a point, nonetheless. Anxiety has made me empathetic; I can sense someone else's unease across a room – the slight tension, the forced smile, the eyes scanning for exits. I can often help, even in small ways.

She's also made me thorough. Nothing slips past me because I've already triple-checked it – contracts, emails, travel arrangements. If there's a detail to miss, I haven't missed it because she's been hovering, making sure I don't.

'You forgot to ...'

'No, I didn't. I already did it.'

'Oh. Good. What about ...'

'Done that too.'

'... Well. Fine then.'

In her twisted way, she's even made me more compassionate with myself. I know how hard this is and how much energy it takes to get through a normal day with her chattering constantly. Every evening I'm still standing is a small victory. Every social event I survive is an achievement. Every morning I get out of bed despite her dire predictions is proof that I'm stronger than I sometimes feel.

THE ADVICE SECTION

(For anyone who recognises themselves in this mess)

If you've read this far and thought, 'Christ, that's me', welcome to the club. It's not a fun club, and there are no T-shirts – but you're not alone. Millions of us are wandering around, doing our best while our brains insist that everything is terrible and getting worse.

Here's what I've learned: take what's useful, ignore what isn't.

1. Stop trying to evict them

Your anxiety isn't leaving. The sooner you accept that you're in a long-term relationship with it, the sooner you can start making that relationship bearable. You wouldn't spend twenty-five years trying to fundamentally change a spouse's personality. It wouldn't work. Same principle here.

2. Name them

Give your anxiety a form, a face, a personality. Separate it from yourself. It's not you; it's something talking to you. That distinction matters more than you think.

3. Set boundaries

You can't make it leave, but you can set rules:

'We're not discussing health concerns between midnight and 7 am.'

'We're not Googling symptoms.'

'We're not rehashing that conversation from six years ago.'

Boundaries will be violated constantly but having them gives you something to point to: 'We agreed. Not now.'

1. Schedule worry time

It sounds ridiculous, but it works. Give your anxiety a dedicated slot – say, twenty minutes at 5 pm – to bring up whatever it wants. Outside that slot, tell it to wait: 'Write it down and we'll discuss it at 5'. Half the time, the worry has dissipated by then; the other half, you handle in a contained way instead of letting it spill across your day.

2. Move your body

Yes, exercise is good for anxiety. No, you don't have to run a marathon – a walk or a swim works. Anything that gets you out of your head and into your body. Your anxiety lives in your mind; your body is enemy territory. Use it.

3. Accept the bad days

Some days, nothing works, and she wins. Some days, you end up in a toilet cubicle, breathing into your hands, convinced everything is falling apart. Those days aren't failure. They don't mean you're back to square one. They're just bad days, and they will pass.

4. Celebrate the good days

Notice and enjoy the days when life feels almost normal. Don't spend them worrying when the good feeling will end – that's her talking. Good days are proof that good days are possible. File them away for the bad days when you need reminding.

5. Get help if you need it

Therapy, medication, admitting you can't do it alone – none of it is shameful. The people who struggle most with anxiety are often those who refuse help, because asking for it feels like weakness. It's not. It's strategy. Your anxiety is formidable; don't face it unarmed.

6. Talk about it

Tell someone. Not everyone, but someone – a partner, friend or therapist. Anxiety thrives in silence and secrecy, convincing you that you're alone and a burden. Bollocks. Millions understand. Saying it out loud – 'I have anxiety, and today it's being a complete arsehole' – takes some power away.

7. Be patient with yourself

This is a long game. No quick fixes. No overnight cure. Just gradual improvement, accumulating good days and learning what works. You'll have setbacks, days that feel like starting over. You're not. Every day you live with anxiety, you're learning – and getting stronger.

THE FINAL WORD

She's sitting with me now as I finish this section, watching me type and occasionally interjecting:

'They're going to think you're mental.'

'Maybe.'

'This is a lot of personal information to share with strangers.'

'Also true.'

'What if no one relates to any of this? What if it's just you?'

Then, it's just me ... but I don't think it is. I believe there are thousands – maybe millions – of people living with their own version of her. Their own anxious lover, paranoid flatmate or cavewoman who never got the memo that the sabre-toothed tigers are extinct.

And I want them to know this: you can live with it. You can have a full, rich, meaningful life with that voice chattering away in the background. It won't be the life you imagined – the one where you're calm, confident and never wake up at 3 am convinced you're dying – but it can still be a good life. Even a funny life. A life with good days, bad days, weird days and days where you find yourself talking to your own brain in a toilet cubicle at a conference.

We're all just muddling through. The anxious ones. The supposedly normal ones (who are probably more anxious than they let on). Nobody really knows what they're doing. We're all just trying to get through the day without completely falling apart.

And if you're reading this, you're doing it. You're getting through – because you're still here.

'For now,' she adds, because she can't help herself.

For now. And that's enough.

ADAM'S ANXICTIONARY

A Glossary of Terms Your Therapist Won't Teach You

Every relationship needs its own language. My wife and I have ours – built over years of shared meals, arguments about whose turn it is to let the dog out and that look she gives me when I've said something spectacularly thick at a dinner party.

Anxiety and I have developed our own vocabulary too.

The English language wasn't built to describe the specific flavours of dread that appear at 3 am, or the horror of realising you've sent an email to 'All Staff' instead of 'Alan from Accounts'. So I've made up new words.

This glossary – an Anxictionary, if you like – contains terms I wish had existed when I was a twenty-two-year-old paratrooper trying to figure out why jumping out of a perfectly good aircraft felt less terrifying than small talk at a regimental dinner. Consider it your field guide to the absurd …

1. Anxietease (anx-EYE-uh-teez) – noun

A nagging worry that flirts with your attention but won't reveal what it's actually about. Emotionally, it's like someone tapping you on the shoulder in a crowd and vanishing before you can turn around.

Example: In a meeting about Q3 projections, your stomach clenches. Something's wrong … but what? Did you leave the oven on? No. Is your mother ill? She seemed fine yesterday. Did you accidentally CC someone dodgy? You've checked seventeen times – it wasn't. Yet anxietease continues its little dance, waving at you from across the room without introducing itself.

Field notes: Anxietease is anxiety keeping you on retainer – like a solicitor who charges by the hour but won't say what case you hired them for. My approach:

'Alright, you mysterious bastard. Either tell me what you want or piss off while I finish this spreadsheet.'

Sometimes it reveals itself. Usually, it just likes being noticed.

2. Anxicrastinate (anx-ih-KRASS-tin-ate) – verb

To delay a task specifically because thinking about it makes you nervous, guaranteeing it becomes more nerve-wracking each hour. The self-defeating art of making your future self absolutely hate your present self.

Example: The tax return sits on your desk unopened for six weeks. You haven't opened the envelope from HMRC because … it exists. Anything inside must be bad news. You create a shrine of avoidance on top of it. Deadline: Thursday. It's Wednesday evening. You are now anxicrastinating about your anxicrastination. You worry about why you're worrying instead of doing the thing.

Field notes: I once anxicrastinated on a medical appointment for so long that the doctor retired before I went. The army trained me to run towards gunfire but never to open a brown envelope within the same calendar year. The cure?

Treat anxicrastinated tasks like ripping off a plaster. Fast, decisive and done.

3. Anxiversary (anx-ih-VER-suh-ree) – noun

The annual return of dread tied to a specific date or event from your past. Your brain's way of celebrating trauma with the enthusiasm of a surprise party you never wanted.

Example: Every 14 March, inexplicable dread hits. Daffodils bloom. Weather improves. And yet, you want to crawl under the duvet until Easter. Then you remember: 14 March 2019 – the redundancy, or the dog's death or that speech at your brother's wedding. Your body has stored the anniversary without consulting your conscious mind.

Field notes: My body remembers dates I don't. It's like having a PA brilliant at scheduling misery. I now greet these anxiversaries with the resignation of a man who knows the in-laws are coming for Christmas.

'Ah, it's you again. Right. Let's get through this together.'

4. Panxiety (pan-ZY-uh-tee) – noun

The particular flavour of worry that arrived around 2020 and never left. A background hum of global dread mixed with fear of other people's respiratory systems.

Example: At a restaurant, someone coughs. Defcon 3. Hand sanitiser deployed. You calculate air circulation, judge the cougher and consider whether your starter is worth the potential viral exposure. It is because of the burrata.

Field notes: Panxiety went mainstream. Government press conferences became its stage. The upside? For two years, general anxiety felt quaint in comparison.

'Oh, worried about your mortgage? That's cute. Have you met my friend Existential Plague Dread?'

5. Anxietude (anx-EYE-uh-tood) – noun

The defensive posture you adopt when someone says, 'Just relax' or 'Try not to think about it'. A cocktail of irritation, vindication and the murderous calm of someone told to smile by a stranger.

Example: A well-meaning colleague notices your tension. 'You know what you should do?'

Anxietude forms like storm clouds over the Pennines.

'You should try meditation.'

Ah yes, meditation. Clearly humanity's long-lost solution to anxiety. Your smile is rigid, eyes dead. Anxietude is fully operational.

Field notes: Anxietude is anxiety defending itself against perceived threats, ironically making you more anxious. Spot it, acknowledge it and try to stand down the emotional troops. Karen probably means well – but telling someone with anxiety to 'breathe deeply' is like telling someone whose house is burning to 'try less fire'.

6. Frenxiety (fren-ZY-uh-tee) – noun

Nervous energy, expressed as manic productivity rather than paralysis. Too anxious to sit still, you clean the house, reorganise socks by colour gradient and finally fix the dripping tap that's been leaking since 2017.

Example: Instead of sitting quietly with your dread while waiting for medical results, you've hoovered the car interior, alphabetised the spice rack and are now seriously considering rewiring the garden shed. Your wife finds you at midnight, installing a new shower head.

'The results come tomorrow,' she says gently.

'I know,' you reply, wielding a wrench like a man possessed, 'but have you seen the water pressure in there? Criminal.'

Field notes: Frenxiety is anxiety's productive cousin. It's the one who shows up to the family reunion having run a marathon that morning and brought homemade chutney. I've built businesses, started companies and written books on the back of frenxiety. The army loved it because it looked like initiative – it was really terror in a beret – but the results were the same.

7. Anxcitement (anx-SITE-ment) – noun

That indistinguishable blend of dread and anticipation before something you actually want to do. Imagine a dog simultaneously excited and terrified by the hoover.

Example: You've been looking forward to a holiday for

months. You've packed sensibly, made lists, researched the hotel and restaurants and planned the optimal time to visit the local ruins for decent lighting.

And now, the night before, you're lying awake at 2 am, absolutely convinced that: (a) you'll miss the flight, (b) the hotel will have burnt down, (c) you'll get food poisoning, (d) the ruins will be underwhelming and (e) somehow, inexplicably, you'll come home worse off than when you left.

This is anxcitement – you can't wait, but you're also dreading it. Same body, different interpretation.

Field notes: The body can't tell the difference between anxiety and excitement. Racing heart, sweaty palms, heightened alertness – they're identical. The difference is software: how you interpret it. I now label anxcitement as excitement whenever possible. 'I'm not nervous about this speech; I'm thrilled my body's preparing me for it.' It's bollocks, of course – but useful bollocks.

8. Doomxiety (doom-ZY-uh-tee) – noun

The compulsive consumption of distressing news, fully aware it's making everything worse. The digital age equivalent of repeatedly poking a bruise to see if it still hurts.

Example: It's 11 pm. You should be asleep, but instead you're reading your fourteenth article about climate change, the economy or the latest geopolitical nightmare.

Each article makes you feel worse, leading to the next, until you're an expert on things you can't influence, control or change. Cortisol levels? Medieval peasant level. But sure – just one more article …

Field notes: Doomxiety seeks certainty in an uncertain world: if I just read enough, I'll understand, I'll be prepared, I'll be safe. Except that's not how it works. News isn't a study guide for life. I've learned to set boundaries: half an hour of news in the morning, then I'm done. My anxiety wants more – but it also wants me to survive until retirement.

9. Socialxiety (so-shul-ZY-uh-tee) – noun

The horror of networking events, work dos and any gathering where you must make small talk while holding a drink and canapé, leaving no hands free to escape.

Example: The company Christmas party. You've been dreading it since September, when Janet first mentioned it in the all-staff meeting. You've prepared conversation topics, identified escape routes, and practised your 'delighted to meet you' face in the mirror – so much so that your wife finally asked if you were having a stroke.

Now you're trapped near the vol-au-vents, and someone from accounts, whose name you really should know, is approaching with clear intent to chat. Your fight-or-flight kicks in. Fleeing would be rude, fighting seems excessive, so you go with the third option: freeze, while internally screaming.

Field notes: Socialxiety convinced me for years that I was an introvert. I'm not; I'm an anxious person who mistook exhaustion from constant internal panic for a need for alone time. These days, I give myself permission to leave events early – which, oddly, makes me stay longer. Just knowing there's an escape hatch makes the room feel less like a prison.

10. Anxietweaks (anx-EYE-uh-tweeks) – noun
Those small, obsessive adjustments you make to something already finished because you can't let it go. The document equivalent of straightening a picture frame seventeen times when it was fine the first time.
Example: The presentation's done. It was done three days ago. Reviewed, approved, praised by colleagues. You're about to present in seven minutes – and yet, there you are in the corridor, phone in hand, changing 'utilise' to 'use' on slide fourteen because suddenly 'utilise' feels wanky and everyone will notice. They won't, but your anxietweaks don't care about probability. They care about the unbearable feeling of imperfection attached to your name.
Field notes: Anxietweaks murdered my first draft of this book. I couldn't stop 'improving' until there was nothing left but a pile of versions and a sense of having made things worse. Now I follow a simple rule: three passes, then done. First pass: content. Second: clarity. Third: polish. After that, I physically remove access to the document. It's done

because I've decided it's done, not because it's perfect. Nothing is ever perfect. My anxiety disagrees, but it's wrong.

11. Retrospanxiety (retro-SPANX-eye-uh-tee) – noun
Worrying about things that have already happened and cannot be changed. Mental time travel solely for the purpose of suffering.
Example: It's 3 am, and you suddenly remember something you said at a barbecue in 2009. 'Nice baps,' you told your colleague's wife, referring to the bread rolls she'd brought. She looked at you strangely. You've never recovered. You never will. And the fact she almost certainly forgot about it within hours is irrelevant. Your brain has preserved the moment in exquisite detail, ready to replay whenever you're vulnerable, knackered or foolish enough to think you might sleep through the night.
Field notes: Retrospanxiety is my brain's favourite hobby. It comes with a greatest hits compilation:

- The time I called my commanding officer 'Mum'
- The job interview where I forgot my own career history
- Every email I've ever sent with a typo.

I've learned to treat these intrusive memories like an elderly relative telling the same story for the hundredth time. 'Yes, brain. I know. Baps … very embarrassing. Can we move on now?'

12. Financxiety (fin-ANKS-eye-uh-tee) – noun
Self-explanatory, universal and chronic: the dread tied to bank balances, bills and the certainty that one unexpected expense will leave you ruined, regardless of your actual finances.
Example: You're doing fine. You know it, the numbers confirm it – but then the boiler makes a worrying new sound. Suddenly, you're catastrophising a scenario where it explodes, insurance refuses to pay, repairs bankrupt you and you end up living in a cardboard box, explaining to passers-by that it all began with a gurgle in the central heating. Your wife points out that boilers make sounds sometimes. You nod – you hear her – but you also hear the cardboard box calling.
Field notes: Financxiety doesn't respond to logic; it's not about money, it's about security – a feeling, not a number. I know people who panic about finances while sitting on small fortunes, and others who are genuinely skint but sleep like babies. Anxiety isn't measuring your bank balance; it's measuring your sense of safety. I've found that even a small 'worst-case scenario' fund helps more than any spreadsheet. It's not the amount that matters – it's knowing it exists.

A NOTE ON NAMING THINGS

This glossary wasn't just an exercise in clever wordplay (though I won't pretend 'anxicrastinate' doesn't make me disproportionately proud). Naming things matters. When you can name something, you can see it more clearly – and when you see it clearly, you can talk about it, understand it and start to manage it.

For years, my anxiety thrived in vagueness. It was a shapeless fog, impossible to navigate. But 'anxietease'? I can spot that. 'Doomxiety'? I know that one too. Naming these experiences turns overwhelming forces into specific visitors with recognisable patterns and predictable behaviours. It also makes them a bit ridiculous – which, as it turns out, is incredibly therapeutic.

Here's the thing about anxiety: it takes itself very seriously, and it wants you to do the same. It arrives like a bureaucrat from a government department, forms in hand, protocols at the ready, dire warnings at every turn. But bureaucrats hate being laughed at. So I laugh – not at myself for having anxiety (that's a mug's game), but at anxiety itself. I laugh at its pretensions, its melodrama and at the sheer absurdity of a brain that can build businesses and run towards danger yet can't open a letter from HMRC without hyperventilating.

Feel free to add your own terms to this glossary. Name your experiences, make them ridiculous, give them daft pronunciations and absurd examples. Your anxiety won't like it – which is precisely the point.

PART FOUR

THE TOOLKIT

(Or practical stuff that actually works, from someone who's tried everything)

CHAPTER NINETEEN

THE TOOLKIT (A LOVE LETTER TO ORGANISED CHAOS)

'You can either look sane and feel insane or look insane and feel relatively okay. I'll take the latter.' – Adam Knights

I know, I know. You've been waiting for the practical bits – the 'what do I actually do' section, the part where I stop wittering on about pink spaghetti mistresses and give you something useful. Well, here it is: my personal toolkit for **loving anxiety instead of fighting it.**

A CONFESSION

This toolkit isn't fixed. It's not laminated and hung on my bathroom wall like some motivational poster with a sunset and the word BELIEVE. It's a living, breathing, constantly evolving collection of techniques. I add to it, steal ideas from others and sometimes abandon methods that stop working.

I've borrowed from therapists, soldiers, business coaches, random strangers on aeroplanes, a wise taxi driver in Manchester and even a children's book about a worried caterpillar my niece left at my house. If it works, it goes in the toolkit. If it stops working, it comes out. No ego. Just pragmatism.

And here's the weird part: I run every new tool past my **pink spaghetti mistress** herself.

I'm serious. Whenever I try a new technique, I pay attention to how she responds. If she goes quiet – not regrouping for a bigger assault – I know I've found a good one.

It's like having a built-in quality control system, except the controller is a neurotic entity of pure catastrophic imagination, living rent-free in my chest.

Take the breathing technique a corporate wellness consultant once taught me: breathe in for four, hold for seven, breathe out for eight, or whatever the numbers were. My anxiety got louder.

'Oh good,' she said. 'Now we're counting. What if you lose count?

What if you're wrong?

What if this is the technique that finally doesn't work, and you're stuck like this forever?'

That one lasted three days before I discarded it. But when I stumbled upon the Float method (more on that in a moment), she went silent. I'd found her mute button. That's when I knew I'd struck gold.

Everything that follows has been **field-tested, anxiety-approved** and refined through years of personal experimentation. Consider me your anxiety guinea pig. I've already had all the panic attacks, so you don't have to. You're welcome.

THE GREETING

What it is: When anxiety shows up, acknowledge it immediately: 'Hello, there you are.' Don't pretend it isn't happening; don't push it away. Just notice it.

Why it works: What you resist persists. Years of trying to slam the door in anxiety's face taught me that the harder you push, the louder she gets.

The story: I was in a high stakes board meeting with venture capitalists, expensive suits, the whole intimidating circus. Anxiety tightened my chest, thoughts spiralled. Normally, I'd push through, jaw clenched, hoping it would pass. It never did.

Exhausted, I tried something different. In my head I said, 'Hello. I know you're here. I see you.'

That's it. No strategy, no breathing technique. Just acknowledgement. Instantly, intensity dropped by about 30 per cent. She'd been banging on the door demanding notice; the moment I opened it; she didn't need to bang as hard.

Now I greet her like an old friend I'm too polite to ignore: 'Oh, hello. You're here. Wonderful. Absolutely wonderful.'

Key: Mean it – or at least pretend convincingly enough to trick yourself. Fake acceptance instead of confidence; somehow both easier and harder.

Dark bonus tip: Sometimes I greet her out loud when alone:

"'Morning, you neurotic spaghetti monster. What fresh hell have you brought me today?'

There's something deeply satisfying about swearing at your own anxiety before she's even settled in. It sets the tone for the day and lets her know who's in charge (it's never me, but she doesn't need to know that).

THE FLOAT

What it is: Instead of fighting sensations, imagine floating on them – like lying on your back in a swimming pool, letting the water hold you up. You don't have to do anything but float.

Why it works: Anxiety triggers your body's ancient fight-or-flight instincts. But here's the thing – there's no sabretooth tiger. Just a meeting, a social event or a phone call you'd rather avoid. Floating is surrender without defeat. You ride the wave instead of swimming against it.

The story: This technique came from a panic attack at a swimming pool. Weeks of poor sleep, no appetite, high anxiety and caffeine-fuelled determination had me exhausted. A friend suggested swimming: 'Exercise releases endorphins'.

I did lengths with military precision. Ten laps in, panic struck in the slow lane, surrounded by elderly women doing breaststroke. I couldn't swim, arms useless, breathing ragged. So I rolled onto my back and floated, staring at the ceiling, expecting to drown. It seemed at least like an interesting obituary story.

I didn't drown. My body knew how to float – I just hadn't let it before. Panic still raged, heart racing, thoughts catastrophising, but I wasn't fighting it. I was floating on top of it. That day, my pink spaghetti mistress went quiet for the first time in weeks.

Now: Whenever anxiety peaks, I imagine floating. Water, space, a supportive cloud – it doesn't matter. What matters is surrender. Release the desperate fight.

Dark bonus tip: In meetings or social situations, when you can't lie down, imagine your body is lighter than air, like helium or marshmallow. Floating works. Bonus: if it's marshmallows, you might get slightly hungry – a manageable side effect.

THE SO WHAT

What it is:

For every catastrophic thought, ask 'So what?' repeatedly until you reach something manageable.

The structure:

- *'What if I have a panic attack?'* So what?
- *'People will stare.'* So what?
- *'It'll be embarrassing.'* So what?
- *'I'll survive embarrassment.'*

Yes. You will.

Why it works:

Because anxiety is essentially a fortune-teller with a relentlessly negative outlook. She specialises in predicting the worst possible outcomes and presenting them as inevitable facts.

The So What technique calls her bluff. It responds with, 'Okay. And then what?' again and again, forcing the catastrophe to run to its natural conclusion. Almost without exception, when you finally reach the bottom, what's waiting there is something survivable.

Anxiety thrives on vagueness and escalation. So What strips both away.

THE STORY BEHIND IT:

I was about to give a presentation to roughly two hundred people at a large conference – the full horror show: big stage, microphone, spotlights and a silent audience waiting to judge me.

My anxiety was having the time of her life.

- *'What if you forget your words?'* she whispered helpfully.
- *'What if your mind goes completely blank?'*
- *'What if you freeze up there and everyone realises what a fraud you are?'*

At the time, I was working with a coach – an ex-military guy with absolutely no tolerance for theatrics. He'd taught me this technique, so, standing backstage with my heart trying to escape my chest, I decided to use it.

'What if I forget my words?'

So what?

'I'll look stupid.'

So what?

'People will think I'm incompetent.'

So what?

'Maybe I won't get invited back.'

So what?

'Maybe my business will suffer.'

So what?

'Maybe I'll have to find other speaking opportunities.'

So what?

'I'll ... find other speaking opportunities?'

Right. And will you die?

'No.'

Will anyone you love be harmed?

'No.'

Will the world end?

'Probably not, no.'

So what, exactly, are we worried about?

By the time I reached the end of the chain, it was obvious that the worst-case scenario amounted to nothing more than a bad day –survivable, forgettable and ultimately insignificant.

I've had hundreds of bad days. I'll have hundreds more. They pass. They always do.

I gave the presentation. It was fine – not my best work

and not my worst. Nobody died and the world continued turning. My anxiety had predicted nuclear apocalypse, and the actual outcome was 'mildly mediocre'.

That's the pattern, by the way. Anxiety forecasts annihilation; reality delivers mild disappointment at worst.

Advanced technique: Sometimes anxiety skips straight to the nuclear option.

'What if you have a heart attack and die?'

This is where you need to be willing to go dark.

'So what if I die?'

Well, I'll be dead, so I won't care. The people I love will grieve and then continue with their lives, because that's what people do. The universe will keep expanding, and my taxes will finally stop being my problem.

There's something strangely liberating about following the catastrophe all the way to its conclusion and realising that even the ultimate worst-case scenario is not worth living in constant fear of. We're all dying anyway. We might as well have some lunch first.

Dark bonus tip: I once played 'So What' with my anxiety about whether people liked me:

'What if literally no one on earth likes me?'

So what?

'I'll be lonely.'

So what?

'I'll get a dog.'

And do you know what? I would. I'd get a dog, and the dog would like me – because dogs are excellent judges of character and because I'd have food.

Problem solved. Existential crisis averted by the hypothetical spaniel.

THE TIME LIMIT

What it is:

Tell yourself the anxiety will pass in twenty minutes – because it usually does. If it doesn't, give it another twenty. The point is to break the 'this will last forever' lie.

Why it works:

Because anxiety's favourite trick is permanence.

'This is your life now. This feeling, forever. You will never feel normal again. You will never feel safe again. This is the new reality, and you'd better get used to it.'

It's bollocks, of course. Anxiety is a wave, and waves pass. But when you're in the middle of one, it's very hard to remember there was ever a time before it – or to imagine a time after.

The time limit is a reminder that this, too, shall pass – usually in about twenty minutes – because that's how long it takes for your nervous system to burn through its adrenaline and calm the hell down.

The story behind it:
I was having a proper panic attack at home – heart racing, convinced I was dying. I called a friend who happened to be a paramedic. She listened carefully, established that I was not, in fact, having a cardiac event, and then said something that changed my life:

'Set a timer for twenty minutes. If you're still dying after twenty minutes, call me back.'

I thought she was being dismissive. Possibly cruel. How dare she reduce my profound suffering to a sitcom-length inconvenience? Did she not understand the magnitude of my distress?

I set the timer anyway – mostly out of spite, just to prove her wrong.

Eighteen minutes later, the panic had faded to a manageable background hum. I was sitting on my kitchen floor, slightly embarrassed, eating a biscuit. The sabre-tooth tiger had revealed itself to be an annoying house cat.

Now, whenever anxiety hits, I give it a time limit.

'You've got twenty minutes,' I tell her. 'Make the most of it. Throw everything you've got at me. After that, we're done.'

Sometimes she takes the full twenty. Sometimes she gets bored and wanders off after ten. Either way, the finiteness makes it bearable. It's the difference between 'I'm trapped in this feeling forever' and 'I'm trapped in this feeling for about as long as a sitcom episode.'

Dark bonus tip: Over time, I've started assigning different time limits to different flavours of panic:

- Normal panic attack – twenty minutes
- Panic triggered by existential dread about the meaninglessness of existence – thirty-five minutes
- Panic triggered by accidentally emailing the wrong person – fortyfive minutes minimum, plus however long it takes to write an apologetic followup email.

The point is to track your patterns and know your enemy. My pink spaghetti mistress has her rhythms. Once I learned them, she became a lot less frightening.

The Body Scan

What it is: Instead of fearing your physical symptoms, get curious about them. Ask yourself: Where exactly is the tightness? How big is it? What colour would it be? What is its texture? It sounds bonkers – but this simple shift transforms fear into curiosity.

Why it works: Anxiety feels terrifying because it's vague and overwhelming.

- 'I feel terrible' is overwhelming.
- 'There's a tennis-ball-sized knot, slightly purple, with the texture of tangled wool, located about three inches below my left shoulder blade' is specific. Now it's manageable. Almost interesting, even.

Curiosity and fear can't occupy the same space. When you focus on investigating something, you can't simultaneously be terrified of it. That's how scientists studying deadly disease function – they replace fear with fascination.

The story behind it: I was training for something – I can't even remember what, some fitness goal – and I'd pulled a muscle in my back. The physiotherapist asked me to lie down and describe exactly where the pain was.

- 'My back hurts,' I said.
- 'Where in your back?'
- 'All of it.'
- 'Point to it.' I pointed to a specific spot.
- 'Good. Now describe it. Sharp or dull?'
- 'Sharp.'
- 'Constant or intermittent?'
- 'Intermittent.'
- 'Like stabbing or burning?'
- 'Stabbing, I suppose.'

By the time she finished interrogating me, I realised something remarkable: it hurt less. Not because she'd done anything physical, but because the investigation itself had defused the experience.

I tried the same approach with anxiety. The next time I felt chest tightness, instead of panicking, I got curious:

- Where exactly is it? Centre of my chest and slightly left.
- How big? About the size of my fist.
- What colour? Dark red, pulsing.

- Texture? Knotted, like a clenched muscle.
- Temperature? Warm. Not hot, just warm.

By the end of this mental 'inspection', the sensation had shifted. It was still there but no longer frightening – just interesting data about what my body was doing.

My anxiety hates this technique … absolutely despises it. Which is how I know it works. She wants my full attention on the terror, not the clinical details. When I start describing her effects like a weather report, she loses interest.

ADVANCED TECHNIQUE: NAMING THE SENSATION

Sometimes I give physical sensations names – not in a spiritual, 'heal your inner child' way, but more in a, 'you're an absolute inconvenience' way. My chest tightness becomes Nigel, my racing heart is Sharon and the stomach knot is Gerald.

'Oh, Gerald's back. Hello, Gerald. About the size of a tangerine today, are we? Slightly green, texture like cold porridge? Wonderful. Carry on.'

It's hard to be terrified of something called Gerald.

Dark bonus tip: This works for other physical symptoms too –headaches, nausea or even that weird clicking in my knee. My body becomes a source of fascination rather than fear. I'm like a naturalist … except the wildlife is my own nervous system.

THE PHONE A FRIEND

What it is: Tell someone how you feel – not to seek reassurance, but simply to say it out loud. 'I'm feeling really anxious right now.' Naming it diminishes its power.

Why it works: Anxiety thrives in secrecy. She wants you to hide her, pretend everything's fine and suffer quietly while everyone assumes you've got it together. Saying her name out loud robs her of control. It's like those fairy tales where knowing a creature's true name gives you power – except your imp is your neurotic brain chemistry, and the spinning wheel is probably a meeting.

A critical distinction: This is not reassurance-seeking. That's when you tell someone and need them to say, 'It's okay' or 'Nothing to worry about'. That may feel good short-term, but it makes anxiety worse over time, creating dependence on external validation.

The phone-a-friend technique is different: you're not asking for solutions, you're just acknowledging reality. You don't need a **response; you just need a witness.**

The story behind it: At another conference (they're rich sources of anxiety material), I was about to have dinner with some very important people. Business cards exchanged, futures decided –classic high-stakes stuff.

I was a mess, couldn't think straight and couldn't even choose a drink – a spiral of anxiety about appearing indecisive. I excused myself to the bathroom and called my wife, who answered expecting an emergency.

'I'm really anxious,' I said.

'I know,' she said.

'I just needed to say it.'

'I know,' she said. 'You've got this. Call me when it's over.'

That was it. No reassurance. No pep talk. Just acknowledgement and a witness. And somehow, that was enough to take the edge off.

I went back to the dinner. Still anxious, but less so, because the act of naming it had taken the edge off. It was like a balloon expanding in my chest – telling someone had let a bit of air out.

Who to call: This is important – because not everyone can handle being a 'phone a friend'. Some will try to fix it, which can make things worse. Some will dismiss it, which also makes it worse. And some will get anxious about your anxiety, which is like inception – but far less fun.

You need someone who can simply say, 'I hear you', and leave it at that. Someone comfortable with discomfort. Someone who understands that you're not asking them to solve anything – you're just naming the demon.

I have three phone-a-friends: my wife, an old Army mate who has heard me say much worse things and my therapist's voicemail, which I use when no one else is available and I just need to hear myself say the words.

Dark bonus tip: If you don't have anyone to call, write it down, say it out loud to an empty room or tell your dog. The point is the same and that's naming it, speaking it, making it external rather than keeping it secret and internal.

I've even left voicemails for myself during particularly bad episodes:

'Hi Adam, it's Adam. I'm anxious right now. The dinner thing. You know the one. Anyway ... just wanted to say it. Speak soon. Bye.'

Later, when I listen to them calm, I think, 'God, that poor bastard.' It's oddly comforting to feel a third-person compassion for my past self.

THE ANCHOR

What it is: Focus on one physical sensation – your feet on the ground, your hands or the texture of an object you're holding. One anchor is enough.

Why it works: Anxiety pulls you out of your body and into your head, into the swirling chaos of what-ifs and catastrophic predictions. The anchor drags you back into the present, to the physical reality of the moment – which is usually far less threatening than the imagined future.

The story behind it: This came directly from my military training, though we didn't call it 'anchoring'. We called it 'tactical awareness' – staying present in high-stress situations to avoid getting yourself or your mates killed. When things got intense, the training kicked in: focus on what's in front of you – your feet, your weapon or the texture of whatever you're holding. One thing at a time.

I didn't realise until years later that it was a grounding technique. I thought it was just how you survived. But it turns out it works just as well for panic attacks as it does for life-threatening situations. Who knew the Army was accidentally teaching mindfulness?

My personal anchors: I've experimented with a lot, and some work better than others.

- **Feet on the ground**: Reliable. Push down slightly, feel the floor push back. It's hard to panic while doing a subtle physics experiment with your feet.
- **Hands:** Always available. Focus on texture, temperature or whether they're sweaty (they usually are).
- **Holding something:** Brilliant. I keep a small coin in my pocket. When anxiety spikes, I explore its ridges, smooth faces and weight. By the time I've fully examined this coin I've carried for seven years, the worst of the anxiety has usually passed.

The mistake people make: Trying multiple anchors at once – feet and hands and breathing and counting and focusing on a distant point and reciting poetry. That's cognitive overload. Just one anchor is enough.

Dark bonus tip: I've made some weird anchor choices in desperate moments …

During one particularly bad flight, I anchored to

the texture of the sick bag in the seat pocket. They have surprisingly detailed textures, those bags.

During a panic attack at a funeral, I anchored to the feeling of my suit jacket against my arms.

And during an anxiety spike in a business meeting, I focused on the pain of biting the inside of my cheek – which worked, though I wouldn't recommend it.

The point is: **any anchor is better than no anchor.** In an emergency, you take what you can get.

THE THANKS

What it is: Thank your anxiety for trying to protect you – and actually mean it.

'Thank you for looking out for me. I've got this.' It sounds ridiculous, but it works.

Why it works: Anxiety, at its core, is a protection mechanism that's just a little over-enthusiastic. It's not trying to ruin your life – it's trying to save it. It just hasn't updated its database since the Pleistocene era when most of its reactions actually made sense.

When you thank it, you acknowledge its purpose, validate its existence and stop treating it as an enemy. Instead, you treat it as an overzealous bodyguard who just needs to be gently told to stand down.

The story behind it: This was the hardest technique for me to accept – and also the most transformative.

I spent years at war with my anxiety, trying to defeat

her, eliminate her, destroy her. Every failed attempt only made her stronger and me more exhausted.

Then a therapist suggested something radical: what if I wasn't supposed to defeat her? What if I was supposed to work with her?

'Thank her,' the therapist said.

'Thank her?' I said. 'She's ruined my life.'

'She's tried to protect you. She's done it badly, but the intention was protection.'

I thought about all the times anxiety had stopped me: social events I'd avoided, opportunities I'd missed, relationships I'd damaged.

And then I thought about why she'd done it. It wasn't to hurt me – it was to protect me, to keep me safe from rejection, failure, embarrassment and harm. Her threat assessment was catastrophically wrong, but her motivation was care.

The first time I thanked her, I cried quiet tears. Years of antagonism dissolved into something softer.

'Thank you,' I said. 'I know you're scared. I know you're trying to protect me. But I've got this. You can stand down now.'

She didn't disappear – because that's not how this works – but she became quieter, less urgent. It was as if she'd finally been heard after years of screaming into the void.

How I phrase it now: It's evolved over time

- Sometimes formal: 'Thank you for your vigilance. I acknowledge the perceived threat and will take it under advisement.'
- Sometimes casual: 'Cheers for the heads up, love. I'll take it from here."'
- Sometimes affectionate: 'You ridiculous pink spaghetti monster. Thank you for giving a shit. Now piss off for a bit.'

The tone matters less than the intention. Anxiety needs to feel acknowledged, validated and heard. Once that happens, she can relax.

Dark bonus tip: When I'm feeling particularly cheeky, I thank her sarcastically:

'Oh, how wonderful, another reminder that I might die at any moment. Thank you so much. Really very helpful. Couldn't have done it without you.'

She doesn't seem to mind. I think she's just happy to be addressed at all.

Bonus Tools (Because the Toolkit Never Stops Growing)

The eight techniques above are my foundation – the ones I reach for first and use so often they're practically muscle memory. But the toolkit is never finished. I'm always adding new tools, testing them, keeping what works and discarding what doesn't.

1. The Cold Water Reset

When anxiety is truly out of control and nothing else works, I run cold water over my wrists, splash it on my face or – if I'm at home and desperate – take a cold shower.

There's science behind this: something about the diving reflex, the vagus nerve and the body's hardwired response to cold. I don't fully understand it, but thirty seconds of cold water can break a panic cycle when nothing else will.

My anxiety despises this technique. She goes completely silent, as if too shocked by the temperature change to continue catastrophising. It's like rebooting a frozen computer – you just need to turn it off and turn it back on again.

2. The Permission Slip

Sometimes anxiety fights against something I'm trying to do – going to a party, making a phone call, sending an email. The harder I push, the harder she pushes back.

In those moments, I give myself explicit permission not to do the thing:

- 'You don't have to go to the party.'
- 'You can cancel the phone call.'
- 'The email can wait until tomorrow.'

The moment I give myself permission to escape, the urge to escape often fades. It's as if anxiety panics because she thinks we're trapped – but the moment she sees an exit, she calms down. And often, because I'm now in that calmer place, I realise I do want to go to the party. I just didn't want to feel like I had no choice.

3. The Past Evidence Review

When anxiety predicts something terrible will happen, I ask her for evidence from my past.

'You think I'm going to humiliate myself in this meeting? Okay. When has that actually happened? Show me the incidents.'

Usually, she can't produce any, or only one or two isolated examples from years ago. This proves that the outcome is rare, not inevitable.

Of course, this doesn't work for genuinely novel situations.

'You've never had a meteor land on you – but that doesn't mean it won't!'

Fair enough. But for recurring anxieties – social disasters, professional failures, health catastrophes – looking at the past is surprisingly reassuring.

4. The Ridiculous Worst Case

This is a twist on the classic 'So what?' technique: instead of following the chain to its logical conclusion, you follow it to its ridiculous conclusion.

'What if I embarrass myself?'

So what?

'People will laugh.'

So what?

'I'll become an internet meme.'

So what?

'I'll be mocked on every platform.'

So what?

'I'll have to change my identity and move to another country.'

So what?

'I'll become a goat farmer in New Zealand.'

So what?

'I'll learn to love goats.'

By the time you reach goat farming, the original anxiety feels absurd – because it is absurd. Most catastrophic predictions are, when followed far enough.

5. The Physical Discharge

Sometimes anxiety is just trapped energy. The body has prepared for fight or flight, and it's frustrated when you're just sitting in a meeting, not fighting or fleeing.

In these moments, I find a way to physically discharge the energy:

- A brisk walk
- Some press-ups in the bathroom (yes, I've done press-ups in toilets at multiple conferences. Not my proudest moment, but it works)
- Shaking my hands out, tensing and releasing muscles
- Anything that gives the body somewhere to put all that adrenaline.

After physical discharge, my anxiety quiets down – probably because the energy was her whole point. She was preparing my body for danger, and once the body has done something with that preparation, she feels satisfied.

How I Test New Tools

When someone suggests a new anxiety technique – which, bless them, happens constantly – I put it through a three-stage testing process:

Stage One: Does it sound completely absurd?

If it sounds reasonable and sensible, I'm immediately suspicious. The best anxiety techniques usually sound slightly mad – but they work.

- 'Just float on the panic' sounds insane.
- 'Thank your anxiety' sounds like something from a bad self-help book.
- 'Run cold water over your wrists' sounds like a Victorian governess recommending a cure for hysteria.

Stage Two: Does it work in the moment?

I test the technique during actual anxiety, not when I'm calm. Any tool can sound good in a relaxed state. The real question is whether it works when I'm genuinely struggling.

Stage Three: Does it shut her up?

This is the ultimate test. After using the technique, I pay attention to my pink spaghetti mistress. If she goes quiet – really quiet, not just plotting her next attack – the tool earns its place in my arsenal.

I've discarded more tools than I've kept: meditation apps that made me more anxious, visualisation exercises that sent my thoughts spiralling, breathing techniques that made me hyperventilate, mantras I couldn't take seriously and crystals that did nothing except sit on my desk looking vaguely decorative.

The toolkit must be personal. What works for me might not work for you – and what works for you might trigger a full-blown episode for me. The only way to find out is to experiment, fail, adjust and experiment again.

The Ongoing Conversation

Here's the truth nobody tells you about anxiety management: it's not a problem you solve once. It's an ongoing conversation – a relationship that requires constant maintenance.

Even after years of using these techniques, I still have bad days. My pink spaghetti mistress sometimes arrives with her full catastrophic orchestra, and I temporarily forget every tool I've ever learned. Some methods stop working, or I need to lean more heavily on certain techniques for a while.

The toolkit isn't a cure – **it's a management system**. Like any system, it requires updating, maintenance and sometimes a full rebuild. That's okay. I'm not trying to eliminate anxiety anymore; I'm trying to live with her, work with her and acknowledge that she's part of me and probably always will be. I just need to make the cohabitation as comfortable as possible.

My toolkit is my way of doing that. It's a collection of negotiation tactics for an entity that can't be reasoned with but can sometimes be managed. It's an evidence file proving that anxiety – no matter how terrifying it feels – is always survivable.

And it grows every day: with every conversation, every book, every random insight from a stranger and every desperate experiment at two in the morning. The toolkit evolves because I evolve, because my anxiety evolves and because life keeps throwing challenges that demand new solutions.

So take what works and leave what doesn't. Build your own relationship with your pink spaghetti mistress – or whatever form your anxiety takes. And if you stumble across a particularly good tool, let me know. I'm always collecting.

The Ruby Slippers Were on Your Feet the Whole Bloody Time

Here's something that might make you laugh – or make you want to throw this book across the room.

After twenty-five years of battling my anxiety – twenty-five years of therapists, breathing exercises, self-help books, medications, meditation apps, cold showers and every other remedy known to man – I finally cracked the code.

And do you know what I discovered? I'd had the answer the whole time.

I was Dorothy. We're all Dorothy. Stumbling around Oz, getting attacked by flying monkeys, nearly murdered by a green woman with questionable anger management skills – all because we didn't realise we were already wearing the magic slippers. We just didn't know how to click the bastards together.

If you haven't seen *The Wizard of Oz*, here's the executive summary:

- Kansas girl gets knocked unconscious by a tornado
- Wakes up in Technicolor
- Accidentally murders a witch with her house
- Steals the dead witch's shoes
- Spends the entire film trying to get home while being chased by the victim's sister, who seems justifiably annoyed
- Along the way, Dorothy picks up new friends: a scarecrow who thinks he's stupid, a tin man who thinks he has no heart and a lion who thinks he's a coward.

Spoiler alert – they're all wrong. The scarecrow is clever; the tin man is emotional as hell and the lion shows more courage than most people I've served with in the Paras. They just couldn't see it in themselves. Sound familiar?

After facing witches, flying monkeys and a frankly manipulative wizard, Dorothy finally learns the truth from Glinda the Good Witch: she could have gone home any time. The ruby slippers had the power all along. All she had to do was click her heels three times and say, 'There's no place like home.'

Dorothy's response is perfect. She's confused, maybe a bit pissed off. She asks Glinda why the hell she didn't mention this earlier.

Glinda's answer?

'Because you wouldn't have believed me. You had to learn it for yourself.'

And that, right there, is the most infuriating – and accurate – description of the anxiety journey I've ever encountered.

Here's the thing about Glinda: she can be whoever you need her to be. Maybe your Glinda is a friend who's survived their own tornado. Maybe they're a partner who holds your hand through the flying monkey attacks. Maybe a colleague, a mentor, a support group or that one person who always knows what to say.

But for most of us, Glinda is probably a therapist.

In my case, she was a proper psychologist – someone who'd spent years studying the human mind and had seen enough anxious messes walk through her door to know that I wasn't special, broken beyond repair or the first person in history to need help after a panic attack in Tesco.

Here's what my Glinda did – not giving me all the answers (she couldn't, because they were already in me) – but showing me that I was wearing the ruby slippers. She helped me look down at my own feet and see what had been there all along. Crucially, she taught me how to use them.

I discovered that falling in love with my anxiety, rather than fighting it, was the key. But I needed someone to show me how to click the slippers, when to click them and what to expect when I finally did.

Your Glinda might look different from mine. They might not have any qualifications. They might not even identify as a 'they'. But somehow, they understand you better than anyone with letters after their name ever could.

The point isn't who they are – it's what they do. They don't rescue you. They don't carry you home. They point at your feet and say:

'You see those? You've had the power all along. Now let me show you how to use it.'

For twenty-five years, I looked outside myself for the solution. I tried to kill my anxiety, medicate it into submission, reason with it, ignore it, outrun it and drink it into silence. And let me tell you –anxiety has an iron liver. It will outdrink you every single time.

I consulted wizards – therapists, doctors, coaches, gurus, even that bloke at the pub who seemed to have all the answers after six pints. I collected mechanisms and companions along the way. Some helped. Many didn't. All of them felt like external solutions to an internal problem.

Then, one day, after years of fighting, I stopped fighting. I looked down at my metaphorical feet and realised I was already wearing the ruby slippers. The power to find peace was in me – and had always been in me. I just needed to learn how to knock the bloody things together.

Here's the bit that might save you a quarter-century of arsing about. Glinda was right. I probably wouldn't have believed her at the start if she'd said:

'Mate, you've already got everything you need. Just stop fighting and start loving your anxiety.'

I would have thought they were off their tits. 'Love my anxiety? The thing that makes me feel like I'm dying in supermarket queues, convinces me everyone I love will abandon me and turns a perfectly good Tuesday into a psychological hostage situation ... You want me to LOVE that?'

Yes. That's exactly what I'm telling you. But here's the difference between me telling you and Glinda telling Dorothy – and that's why I wrote this book. You don't need twenty-five years to figure out what took me twenty-five years to learn. I'm handing you the instruction manual for the ruby slippers.

You don't defeat anxiety. You don't overcome it. You don't conquer it, crush it or leave it behind in Oz while you fly off to Kansas. You bring it home with you.

In my version of the story, Dorothy clicks her heels, opens her eyes and she's back in Kansas. The tornado damage is being cleared. Auntie Em is fussing. Toto is being a dog. Everything is grey, familiar and beautiful. Sitting next to her on the farmhouse porch, sipping lemonade like it belongs there – is her anxiety.

It's not gone. It hasn't been defeated or left behind. It's present, acknowledged and accepted.

'Bit of an adventure wasn't it?' the anxiety says.

'Yeah,' Dorothy replies. 'Thanks for trying to keep me safe, even when you were being a complete nightmare.'

'That's my job. I'll probably be a nightmare about other things too.'

'I know. But we're in this together now.'

They sit there, watching the Kansas sunset – two parts of the same whole finally learning to coexist. That's what the ruby slippers really do. They bring you home to the version of yourself that includes anxiety as a passenger, not a hijacker.

You've been wearing these slippers your entire life. The power to find real peace – not the absence of anxiety, but freedom within –has always been yours. You just need someone to show you how to click them together. That's what the rest of this book is for. Now, let me show you how to get there.

The Relapse Myth

Here's something no one tells you: there's no such thing as relapse.

You'll have bad days, bad weeks and maybe even bad months. You'll have moments where you think, 'I'm right back where I started. Nothing has changed. I'm broken forever.'

You're not.

Every time you practise accepting anxiety instead of fighting it, you're building a new neural pathway. You're teaching your brain a different response. And neural pathways don't disappear just because you hit a rough patch.

A bad day isn't a failure. It's practice.

One bad day doesn't erase all the good ones. One panic attack doesn't mean you've forgotten how to cope. One sleepless night doesn't mean you'll never sleep again.

Progress isn't linear, and anyone who tells you otherwise is selling something.

Getting Things in Proportion

Here's something that will either terrify you into action or send you straight to the biscuit tin for comfort eating. Possibly both.

I discovered this particular nugget of existential joy during a particularly aggressive bout with my pink spaghetti mistress, when she was absolutely insisting that the email I'd sent three hours earlier – the one with the slightly ambiguous sign-off – was definitely going to end my career, my marriage and possibly Western civilisation as we know it.

So I did what any rational former paratrooper would do.

I started doing maths.

Not the useful kind. The deeply unsettling kind that makes you question every decision you've ever made about how you spend your Tuesday afternoons.

The Brutal Arithmetic of Being Alive

Let's start with the headline figure, shall we?

According to the Office for National Statistics, the average British bloke can expect to live about 79.1 years, and women about 83. The fairer sex, it seems, is rewarded for putting up with us.

That's roughly 4,120 weeks if you're male, or 4,316 weeks if you're female.

Four thousand weeks. That's it.

If your life were a book, you'd already be several chapters in – and let me tell you, some of those early chapters were absolute rubbish.

But wait because it gets worse.

You don't actually get 4,000 weeks of conscious, useful life. Oh no. The universe has other plans for roughly a third of your time on this spinning rock.

The Sleep Tax

Research from Dreams – the bed company, not the anxiety-induced kind we all enjoy at 3 am – found that the average person spends around twenty-six years sleeping. That's 9,490 days, or 227,760 hours.

One third of your entire existence, completely unconscious.

But here's the kicker: we also spend roughly seven years trying to get to sleep.

That's 2,555 days of lying in the dark, wondering if you remembered to lock the back door, replaying that stupid thing you said at Sarah's wedding in 2007 and mentally composing emails you'll never send. My pink spaghetti mistress absolutely loves this time.

So that's thirty-three years – a full third of your life – dedicated to either being unconscious or desperately wishing you were.

What's Actually Left? (Spoiler Alert: Not Much)

Add it all up, and roughly 65–75 per cent of your life is already spoken for, leaving maybe twenty or twenty-five years of genuine, discretionary, do-what-you-want time.

If you're in your fifties like me, a decent chunk of that is already in the rearview mirror – spent on questionable haircuts, failed relationships and decisions you'd probably rather forget.

Twenty years. That's 1,040 weeks. 7,300 days. 175,200

hours of actual living. And yet, here we are, still agonising over that slightly ambiguous email sign-off ...

The Conversation With My Pink Spaghetti Mistress

When I first did the maths, I thought it might send me into a tailspin. More ammunition for the anxiety artillery, surely: 'Look at all this time you've wasted! Look how little is left! PANIC NOW!'

But something strange happened. When I sat down with my pink spaghetti mistress and showed her the numbers, she went quiet. For once, I had the floor.

'Look,' I said, 'we've got maybe 175,000 hours of actual living left. You want to spend 6,000 of those worrying about whether Dave from accounts thinks I was too curt in my Teams' message? Really? That's your priority?'

She shuffled uncomfortably. No answer.

'Because here's the thing,' I continued, smugly, 'I'm going to spend a third of my remaining time unconscious anyway. Another chunk will go on sitting in traffic, standing in queues and watching programmes I'm not even enjoying because I can't find the remote. Do you really think the best use of what's left is catastrophising about a presentation that twelve people will sit through while checking their phones?'

The perspective shift was profound. Not because my anxiety disappeared – she's far too persistent for that – but because I finally had something to negotiate with: a shared understanding of scarcity.

The Sobering Truth That's Actually Quite Liberating

Here's what I've learned from staring at these numbers: most of what we worry about doesn't deserve the time we give it. We have roughly 4,000 weeks. We'll sleep through 1,400 of them, work through another 500–700 and spend 400 staring at screens.

What's left is precious, finite and irreplaceable.

When you sit with that reality, suddenly the email with the ambiguous sign-off matters a lot less. The presentation that might not go perfectly is less critical. And the opinion of someone you'll probably never see again at a party you didn't even want to attend? Practically irrelevant.

My pink spaghetti mistress still shows up – she always will. But now, when she starts catastrophising about things that won't matter in a year, I can point to the numbers and say:

'I've only got so many hours left on this planet, love. And I refuse to spend them worrying about whether someone on the Internet disagrees with me.'

She usually grumbles – but she backs down because even anxiety can't argue with arithmetic.

At the end of the day, it's not the years in your life that count. It's the life in your years.

The Practical Application: The 10,000 Hours Test

When my anxiety starts catastrophising now, I use a little system I call the '10,000 Hours Test'. It goes like this:

Identify the worry. Let's say it's a presentation next week.

Ask: 'In 10,000 hours, will this matter?' That's just over a year from now.

If the answer is no, ask: 'How many of my precious remaining hours am I willing to dedicate to worrying about this?'

Set a worry budget. Fifteen minutes. An hour. Whatever feels proportionate. Then move on.

It doesn't eliminate the worry, but it gives you a framework for negotiation:

'Yes, pink spaghetti mistress, I hear your concerns about this minor workplace interaction, and I'm allocating seventeen minutes to consider the worst-case scenarios. Then we're done. Because I have 175,200 hours left, and I refuse to spend 4,000 of them replaying conversations in the shower.'

PART FIVE

THE LETTERS

(Or things I wish I'd known and things I wish I'd said)

WHAT MY ANXIETY TAUGHT ME

Here's the thing I never expected: anxiety made me a better person.

I know … bear with me.

Before anxiety, I thought I was invincible. I was in the Parachute Regiment, a successful businessman – nothing could touch me – and my ego was roughly the size of a small planet.

Then anxiety arrived. And it humbled me. It showed me that no amount of success, toughness or money could protect me from my own nervous system. It forced me to slow down, to pay attention to my body and to admit that I wasn't superhuman after all.

It also made me more empathetic. Before anxiety, I didn't understand mental health struggles. I was one of those 'just get over it' types. Now I know better. Now I know that the brain is an organ, and like any organ, it can malfunction. That's not weakness – it's biology.

Anxiety taught me patience: with myself and with others. It taught me that strength isn't the absence of fear, but the willingness to keep going despite it. It showed me that the things we resist persist, and the things we accept release their grip.

Would I choose to have anxiety? No. Christ, no. But would I trade everything it has taught me? Also no.

A LETTER TO YOU

Dear reader,

If you've made it this far, you probably know anxiety intimately. You know the midnight terror and the daytime dread. You know what it's like to feel afraid of your own body, to question your own mind and to wonder if you'll ever feel normal again.

I'm not going to promise you that loving your anxiety will cure it, because it won't. Nothing will, probably. Some of us are simply wired this way, and no amount of positive thinking or deep breathing will completely rewire a nervous system.

But here's what I promise you: it can get better. Not perfect – but better. The nights can get easier. The symptoms can become less frightening. The fear of fear can fade. And you can live a full, rich, meaningful life with anxiety as an occasional companion rather than a constant captor.

The path isn't through fighting. I tried that, and it doesn't work. The path is through acceptance, through acknowledgement, through the strange alchemy of treating your anxiety with kindness instead of hostility.

You've survived every panic attack you've ever had.

Every sleepless night. Every moment when you were certain you were dying. You're still here – still reading, still breathing. Your track record is 100 per cent. Don't forget that.

With love and shared understanding,
Adam Knights
PS If it helps, picture me in Tesco, numb-legged, whispering to my anxiety. You're not alone in the absurdity.

WHAT COMES NEXT?

(Or the bit where I admit I still have no bloody idea)

So here we are.

This is the part where I'm supposed to wrap everything up with a neat little bow, hand you a diploma in anxiety management and send you off into the sunset armed with all the answers.

I'm not going to do that.

Partly because life doesn't work that way.

Partly because anxiety certainly doesn't work that way.

But mostly because I'd be lying if I pretended I had it all figured out. I don't.

After twenty-five years of living with this thing – fighting it, wrestling it into corners and eventually learning to walk alongside it – I still wake up some mornings and think, Oh bollocks. Here we go again.

Here's the first thing you need to know about what comes next: your anxiety isn't going anywhere.

What changed wasn't the anxiety. What changed was my relationship with it.

And that's what next looks like.

Not a cure.

Not a finish line.

But a relationship. An ongoing negotiation between you and this ridiculous pink spaghetti ball that will likely continue for the rest of your life.

I'm still here.

Still walking with my anxiety.

Still telling that uninvited salesman to call back later when he turns up at the door.

And here's the thing – what comes next might surprise you.

It certainly surprised me.

With love,
from me and my anxiety.
Same time tomorrow.

EPILOGUE

THE TAP ON THE SHOULDER

Last Tuesday, at 3:47 am, my anxiety tapped me on the shoulder.

My heart was racing. There was that familiar tightness in my chest and the unmistakable sense that something was terribly wrong. I lay there for a moment, assessing. Then I smiled.

'Morning,' I said. 'You're here early.'

I got up, made a cup of tea and sat in the dark kitchen for a while. I let the anxiety do its thing. I didn't fight it. I didn't fear it. I just sat with it, the way you sit with an old friend who needs to talk.

After about fifteen minutes, it faded. Not completely gone, but quiet enough. I went back to bed and slept until morning.

That's the relationship now.

The anxiety still comes – and probably always will – but it doesn't own me anymore. We've reached an understanding, my anxiety and me. A kind of peace. Not the peace of absence, but the peace of acceptance.

The tap on the shoulder still happens. But now, instead of dread, there's something else.

Almost affection.

'Hello, old friend,' I say.

'What's on your mind tonight?'

A FINAL THOUGHT

The irony isn't lost on me that I've written a book about accepting anxiety, and there's a decent chance some anxiety showed up while I was writing it.

That's okay.

It was here. I noticed it. We worked together. That's practice – not perfection, just practice.

So now, close this book. Take a breath. And the next time your anxiety taps you on the shoulder, try something different.

Say hello.

You might be surprised what happens next.

— THE END —

ABOUT THE AUTHOR

Adam Knights is a former member of the Parachute Regiment, a serial healthcare entrepreneur and a man who spent far too long fighting his own nervous system.

He lives in the UK with his anxiety, who declined to be interviewed for this book but sends her regards.

REFERENCES

Office for National Statistics. (2024). National life tables: Life expectancy in the UK, 2022–2024. Available at: ons.gov.uk

Dreams UK. (2024). Your life in numbers: How we spend our time. Available at: dreams.co.uk/sleep-matters-club
National Bed Federation. (2025). Brits spend 27 years in bed on average during their lifetime. Available at: bedadvice.co.uk

YouGov. (2022). The YouGov sleep study: Part one – sleeping patterns. Available at: yougov.co.uk

Geberit AquaClean & National News. (2012). Nearly a year of our life is spent in queues. Survey of 2,000 British adults.

Our World in Data. (2020). Time use: How do people spend their time? Available at: ourworldindata.org/time-use

Gettysburg College. (2020). One third of your life is spent at work. Research summary citing approximately 90,000 lifetime work hours.